A Primer for Spiritually

Thinking Educators

A New "Organic-Living" Translation of Rudolf Steiner's
Original Essay "Education of the Child" with Study Manual

2

To order copies go to: www.Waldorfbooks.com

To contact the author: www.organicthinking.org

Cover by Jean Riordan who also did the cover for An Outline of A Renewal of Waldorf Education. This cover illustrates the energetic form of the renewed human being that has experienced catharsis deep into the skeleton, i.e., beyond the organs and muscles. Aspects of Steiner's written work can provide support for this process; however, a special training is necessary. Noa has developed this empathic, clearing process for all who are willing.

Table of Contents

Background to this Edition … p. 5
Author's Note to CWG Reader's …p. 6
What is Organic, Heart-Thinking? … p.7
A Primer for Spiritually Thinking Educators … P.15
Synopses of the Thirteen Sections … p. 62
Synopses of the Sixty-Five Paragraphs … p. 64
Picture of the Paragraph Synopses 6-10 … p.67
Picture of the Catchword Diagram 6-10 … p. 68
The Study Guide … p.69
The Preface and Second Appendix to the Philosophy of Freehood … p87
Miscellaneous Notes … p.92
Bibliography … p. 95

Walsch: I wish - oh how I wish – that there were schools such as the ones you describe!

God: There are some which *seek to approach* this model.

Walsch: There are?

God: Yes. Read the *writings* of the man called Rudolf Steiner. Explore the methods of the Waldorf School, which he developed.

<u>Conversations with God</u>, Book 2, Neale Donald Walsch

Background to this Edition

With this booklet, I wanted to help those who were unfamiliar with Rudolf Steiner "organic-living" style and meditation by providing an English translation that captured accurately Steiner's paragraph- and sentence-count, syntax, and grammar. Americans have not been able to experience Rudolf Steiner's special style of writing that lives in climb and swoop, in waves. Although an American George O'Neil discovered and outlined Rudolf Steiner manner of writing, his work never had a solid foothold here in the U.S. I see this translation as my first attempt at popularizing George's approach to reading Steiner. By mastering the thought-form, thought-waves contained in A Primer for Spiritually Thinking Educators may you enjoy the high and pleasure that comes from this communing in thought-streams.

*

This text originally appeared in the German Theosophical Society magazine, *Lucifer-Gnosis*, as Die Erziehung des Kindes im Lichte der Geisteswissenschaft. Rudolf Steiner edited and published it as a pamphlet in 1909 with the same title, but changed some of the paragraphs and therewith the form of the essay; and again in 1918 when he republished it for the third printing. I chose to translate the 1909 edition because it has a very regular form and is ideal for group study. The significance of the form will become clear later on.

The original English translation title was The Education of the Child in the Light of Spiritual Science, which I changed to A Primer for Spiritually Thinking Educators. Steiner's work should serve all educators, including those outside of Waldorf education. I changed the title, kept the original edition's vocabulary such as "Theosophical" instead the more modern term "Anthroposophical" as most translators do. I carefully numbered the paragraphs, made spaces for synopses, and added a study guide. Educators connected to Waldorf, Heart-light, Montessori, or Indigo Children schooling may find A Primer invaluable to their work. I believe that the essay speaks to those interested in pioneering an education founded on spiritual concepts.

Educators will be enlivened by this text and forever receive new inspiration in their work. Steiner's organic-living thoughts serve as an outline for anyone looking for a *plastic form* around which they may create their own unique cultural, ethnic, and educational ideal. It was written in a spiritual heart-thinking style, the same thought-patterns, according to Steiner, that all godly inspired texts have at their basis.

*

This booklet has three main parts: the Introduction, A Primer for Spiritually Thinking Educators, and a Study Guide to Heart-Thinking with an overview on how to read Steiner's organic form-work. This booklet, especially the wording and editing of the translation, was a group effort. I can't thank Astrid Riccio, Malte Dierchen, Helena Fitzpatrick, Gerald Reilly, and Amanda Moon enough for their patience, suggestions, and corrections. It would be great if future translation projects would find so many individuals ready to devote their time to the Being of the Heart-thinking.

Author's Note to CWG Readers

It is important to address the Conversations with God (CWG) books written by Neale Donald Walsch because of their inner connection to Rudolf Steiner. The basic themes of Walsch's books one finds in Rudolf Steiner's work; however, Walsch brings spiritual truth and wisdom to light in a popular American idiom. The kinship between these two authors is clear to anyone who has studied them carefully. I believe that Walsch has put much of the essence of Steiner's Anthroposophical wisdom in a new form which is very appropriate for our times.

In Conversations with God, Book 2, God tells Walsch to read Rudolf Steiner's educational writings in order to find a model which *seeks to approach* an ideal form of educating, but that Waldorf itself is not the model attained! Steiner is difficult to read and I imagine that Neale and the Heartlight movement (Heartlight is the school movement attempting to work out of the CWG books) were disheartened in their endeavor to follow up on God's suggestion. What could have been an interesting synthesis – combining Waldorf theory and methods with CWG training and suggestions for modernizing the curriculum – ended in the Heartlight folks incorporating educational models which do not seem to reflect the strivings of Rudolf Steiner, CWG and other spiritually based philosophies.

Steiner's essay, A Primer for Spiritually Thinking Educators, provides what is missing in Heartlight, Sudbury, and other types of education which have as their leitmotif clichés such as "we seek to educate the whole child" or "we want self-directed learners." A Primer outlines the educational tasks of each life period, and gives suggestions which are in harmony with recent scientific brain research and child developmental experts such Joseph Chilton Pearce. Rudolf Steiner started with a whole picture of the human life, and from his picture developed curricula and methods which he saw as strengthening the child in his or her path. Other educators start from an ideology such as "democracy," which sounds nice, but doesn't take into account the priority of knowing the developmental tasks of life. Many of these pedagogical directions emphasize aspects of Steiner's picture: Sudbury understands the importance of functional learning as well as a child's need to learn when *they* are ready; Walsch, Goleman, and Heart-math understand the importance of teaching real emotional education as a main subject, and not simply in an occasional workshop.

Education will only advance to the extent educators have advanced. Instituting the nine principle of "Creation Education" (Tomorrow's God, p.311) requires an intimate knowledge of how the child grows, and of what activities bring out children's innate capacities. The CWG books are essential to the training of new thinking teachers. However, we need true educational know-how before we can talk and teach spiritual abstractions. For a Heartlight teacher to tell a five year old child that "we are all One with everyone and the whole universe" - while the teacher himself does not *live* this principle - would have no educational effect whatsoever. Steiner makes clear that children before the age of seven learn through imitation, and that all *preaching* would be detrimental to the child.

Rudolf Steiner provides a sound skeleton of ideas upon which a new educational body can be formed. The organic form of Steiner's writings supports the type of dynamic thinking which the CWG books *also* contain. Walsch's CWG Volume One is written in organic heart-thinking form; I am sure unbeknownst to the author. A Primer for Spiritually Thinking Educators can be seen as providing a method for practicing the ideals of Creation Education, and the form of the essay provides a systematic explanation of what a true spiritual writing style is.

What is Organic, Heart-Thinking?

My impulse in translating the <u>A Primer for Spiritually Thinking Educators</u> was to introduce readers to Steiner's organic thought-forms and heart-thinking method. I thought I could inspire educators into practicing heart-thinking meditations by providing this new translation and study guide. The pleasure I experienced in studying and practicing it in groups I wish to share with others.

Teachers should have the opportunity to practice a meditation suitable to their task, and from which they can draw strength for their work. (Steiner wrote many books. There is nearly one for every interest.) Waldorf educators, as well as other new-age educators, can now practice the heart-meditation using a text which accurately captures Steiner's unique thought-waves.

Steiner's essay consists of sixty-five paragraphs. One can divide the text into halves: the first half discusses educational reform and the spiritual view of the human being (his energy bodies); and the second half presents educational suggestions based on this view covering the first fourteen years of life. The mid-point of the essay, the thirty-third paragraph, has as its theme the birth of the child, thus dividing the essay into two *moods*: the outer (educational reform and the spiritual view of man), and the inner (the inner nature and psychology of the child). The sixty-five paragraphs can be further subdivided into thirteen groups of five paragraphs, with a new theme being covered in each group.

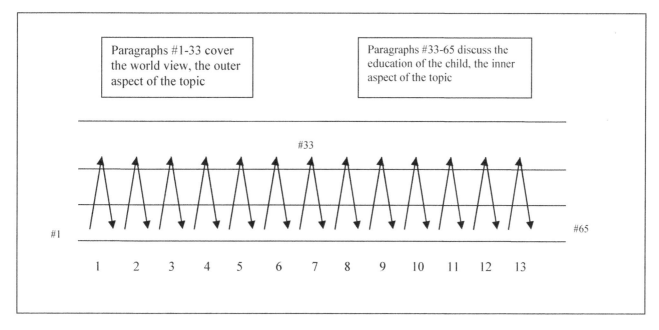

The wave-forms provide a lengthy dream-like meditation of the entire content of the essay. One could ask: "why would I meditate on the form if I have already read and understood the content?" The best reply is: *these forms, the placement and relationship of the thoughts, and their artistic clarity awaken higher feelings and capacities*. In group work, the participants should experience themselves bonding in new ways because of the wave-forms, not in spite of them.

The most effective method is to read and make synopses of each paragraph. One transfers the synopses further onto diagrams or pictures which serve as a musical score for the meditation. Then one studies the thoughts as they climb and swoop through the scales of the heart-thinking. The final stage is to meditate on the whole essay without any diagrams or study notes, moving freely through the energy creating heart-thinking waves.

The Organic Method of Thinking: Steiner's main contribution to spiritual thought consists not only in the fact that he reintroduced reincarnation, spiritual evolution, and meditation back into Western thought, but that he introduced a spiritual-dynamic form of writing. Steiner called this style of writing a "logic of the heart" or organic-living thinking. His goal was to present spiritual truths in such a way that the form in which they were written would enliven the content. Steiner thought that by treating a topic from many systematic points of view that the readers would find themselves being elevated into higher states of awareness.

The form of the writing and thinking of Steiner's logic of the heart is to be found in the sections, paragraphs, and sentences of the essay. Each section has wave-like structures in which the reader goes through expansions and contractions, climbs and swoops like in a cardiogram. The writing style imitates certain organic processes like the beat of a heart, the breathing process, and even the double-helix structure of life itself. As we begin to think in an organic-living, or spiritual manner, we change and open ourselves to new possibilities in life, relationships, and ways of seeing.

The first step in studying Steiner's essay is to practice viewing it from the whole to the parts. Because of the density of his writing style, taking notes and observing how each section relates to the next becomes essential to understanding his message. Surveying this essay from the whole to the parts prepares you for the organic perspectivism practiced in group study.

The logic of the heart is by its own nature a multi-leveled logic. The logic of the heart expands our ability to see things in new ways, ways which challenge our habitual nature. We feel secure with the familiar. A multi-leveled perspectivism allows us to climb systematically and gradually out of what we know, and enter into other points of view. We know what a plant is, but it is hard for us to imagine that a seed becomes a plant, or that a flower is a highly differentiated leaf, or that a fruit is a fat thick leaf. All the stages of the plant belong to and make up the plant, and in order to "know" the plant we need to "know" all of its stages at once. We are required to think of the plant on four levels (as well as Steiner's organic writing), as will be shown later on.

Group Study: There are many different types of study groups: bible groups, Shakespeare groups, book clubs, and great books clubs. Their purpose and intensity differ in degree of preparation, frequency of meeting, etc. Steiner wanted individuals to read his books in order to open their hearts by changing their thought-patterns. Group study, using a text composed with organic-living thinking, brings the readers into a completely new relationship to the levels of being.

Group study means, in this Steinerian sense, a communing with ideas. The group presents the content, puts it into diagrams, rephrases and rewrites the text with the intent of experiencing the text as a living thought-organism. This is a very intense activity. When we reproduce organic thoughts in a group setting, a certain healing power becomes manifest in the group: the power of love.

It seems that group study, especially with spiritual texts, remains an American tradition (note the growth of A Course in Miracles and Conversations with God.). One finds, however, that many of these groups really stay on the surface of the text. Unfortunately this has been the case with the majority of Steiner readers (found in the worldwide branches of the Anthroposophical Society) and even those rare groups which attempt to penetrate deeper into his work; the groups rarely have a feeling for organic form. The goal as outlined in this book can be an integral part of social hygiene in the same way as organic food, exercise, and other holistic activities.

The Individual and the New Consciousness: There are so many tools of transformation available to us today. People are seeking self-transformation. On the Oprah show we see Eckhart Tolle, the author of The Power of Now, Neale Donald Walsch the author of Conversations with God, and many of the famous near-death-experience authors. Their message is the same: human beings must transform their thought-patterns, assumptions, and behaviors. Their books suggest we replace faulty notions, expectations, and beliefs with healthy, correct, power enhancing ones (Louise Hay). They work in the realm of affirmations and changing certain foundational thoughts. Since change does not come easy, these authors provide workbooks and intensive workshops. Walsch calls this process of putting ideals into practice, "holistic living."

Steiner's new form of meditative activity, in my opinion, is the originary holistic thinking. In studying Steiner's form of thinking, the work of others is easily integrated and put into practice. An individual with an organic dynamic form of thinking schooled for example using this essay, A Primer for Spiritually Thinking Educators, learns to work in life organically. By immersing ourselves in organic thought we learn to recognize it in the world (Hegel called it the "godly logic"). True holistic education requires a person who understands life on all levels; this is the main purpose of studying this text.

What about Anthroposophy and Waldorf Education: Rudolf Steiner's work finds its organized form in the Anthroposophical Society headquartered in Dornach, Switzerland. About 40,000 dues paying members live throughout the world. Many large cities especially in Europe have a "branch" or a Steiner study group.

There are several popular impulses from Steiner's work such as Waldorf education and Waldorf teachers colleges, Biodynamic farming and institutes (a variant of organic farming), Anthroposophical medicine, and Camp Hills (care for the mentally handicapped). Less known in the U.S. are the Eurythmy and speech schools, and the "Steiner church" (the Christian Community) priest training. Waldorf education has been the most successful of Steinerian endeavors and one sees the brilliant achievement – in particular the Waldorf schools in Germany with their beautiful buildings, arts and theater, metal work, and orchestras! The leaders of Waldorf education in Europe and abroad are members of Anthroposophical Society.

Unfortunately, the Anthroposophical Society does not recognize Steiner's organic method of thinking and his books are still read solely for their content. The translations done by the various Steiner presses do not take into account Steiner's organic style, but instead, they translate his work in an interpretative manner; sometimes to the point of dumbing down the texts. (Even when they number Steiner's the paragraphs they do it incorrectly!) I was told that Steiner himself indirectly dissolved the Anthroposophical Society (by purposely not appointing a new president) somehow knowing that his followers would slavishly imitate him with little creativity or progress. The Anthroposophical Society is stagnant and declining, which is a shame for Waldorf education because it has lost its source of inspiration. The future may depend on outsiders bringing their inspiration to Steiner's work which has never had a chance to unfold itself fully.

As a possible result of the static nature of the Anthroposophical Society, the Waldorf movement is vigilant in adhering to the standards of the original 1919 school. Many of the Waldorf leaders, however kind and well-intentioned, live in old school Anthroposophy and have not developed the capacities Steiner (or Walsch for that matter) said are necessary for the new educational task at hand. One could argue in their defense that conservative parents do not want their children to learn anything spiritual in school, and to deviate from the 1919 model might mean that Waldorf would lose its integrity. Unless Anthroposophical institutions expand their current purpose and activity they will continue to provide only cursory spiritual practice and healing work.♠

About Form and Content: The form of Steiner's writings is based on a four-level system of perspectives and polarities. The *basic* model Steiner gave was the picture of the seven fold human being in Theosophy. Each member has a different quality or energy level. The base level is the physical level and it has a static, material quality answering the question what?; the life level or etheric level, has a dynamic, living, time-, flowing, process quality, and answers the question how?; the feeling or astral level reflects more human consciousness/feeling and represents a design, intention, desire, function level and quality answering the question why?; the ego or ideal level, is essentially the individual or the thinking level and is in some ways the most elusive level, answering the question who?

Polar to the physical, etheric, astral qualities are the spirit self, life spirit, and spirit man. These three polar aspects of the human being represent the higher energy bodies which the human being creates out of the original three by purifying them with his "I". For example, when the I immerses itself in higher ideas or exercises self-control over his passions the astral body is ennobled into a higher energy field called the spirit self. Although the process is different, the I also works on the physical and etheric bodies turning them into the life spirit body and the spirit man energy field. These seven bodies and their enhancements (movement up and down the four levels) and polarities form the pattern for organic thought sequences as the diagram below illustrates:

♠ Outside of Steiner's basic books, Theosophy and Philosophy of Spiritual Activity, Waldorf teachers colleges would best serve their students by reading and practicing The Four Agreements, and Conversations With God (both come with accompanying study guide books), Dr. Michael Ryce's books in particular the "forgiveness" sheets, and Louise Hay's You Can Heal Your Life. These special books provide a sound basis for a new spirituality and are true modern day Anthroposophy.

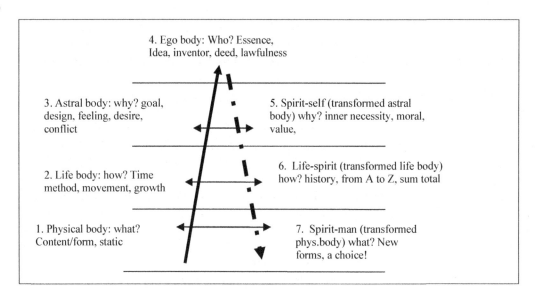

The form of the paragraphs of <u>A Primer for Spiritually Thinking Educators</u> is a series of 13 groups of five paragraphs or in other words paragraphs 1 through 5 make up one theme, 6 through 10 the next theme etc. The theme changes in every group and the groups themselves make a 13-form spanning the four levels. The paragraphs are placed within the four levels, build two interconnected 7-forms, and this is a very abstracted view of the essay.

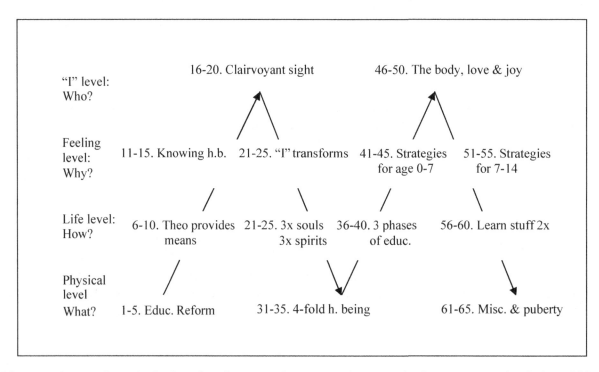

If we continue to focus in further, then for example we can take note of enhancement and polarity within the first 5 paragraphs. The first five paragraphs of the essay (the fractions 1/7 refer to the paragraph number and sentence count thus 1/7 means paragraph number one has seven sentences, 2/5 means paragraph two has five sentences etc.) in synopsis form appear as follows:

1/7 The present age has many questions and many viewpoint from which they answer them.
2/5 The reformers address problems with means which are inadequate; reformers don't understand life.
3/5 Life is like a plant and the observer must learn its hidden nature i.e., the hereditary factors.

4/8 Human life can be known by penetrating inner nature of the human being.
5/2 All reform ideas are fruitful if based on a deeper understanding of human life.

Synopsis of 1-5. "The present age's reform movements require a deeper knowledge of human life."
 Put into diagram form, the synopses build the following organic thought structure:

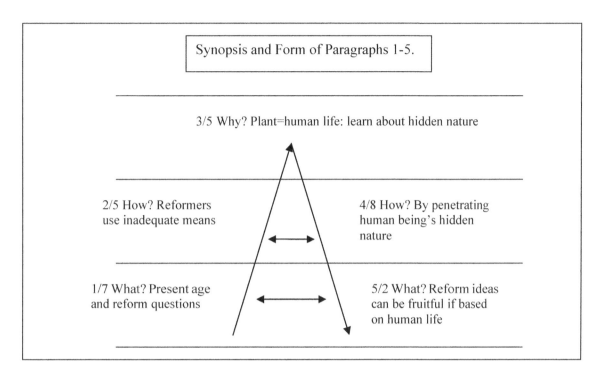

Keep in mind that polarities and enhancements are usually very subtle "answers" to the questions (What? How? Why?), and sometimes nothing more than the inner gestures of the qualities. However, in this case paragraphs 1/7 (what?) and 5/2 (what?) we see that "reform questions" of paragraph 1/7 receive their "fruitful" answer in paragraph 5/2 that is, reforms based on true human life. In 2/5 (how? inadequate means) the problem is stated, while in 4/8 (how?) we see the solution, penetrating the human beings hidden nature.

 The same principles work on the sentence level. In fact one sees in *this* particular essay that Steiner's polarities and enhancements at the sentence level are more exact than at the paragraph level. (The reader will see this especially in many of the curves at the paragraph level in the sense that they don't lend themselves with ease to organic schema.) Below is paragraph 1/7 with *synopses in the parentheses*, and below that, is the organic form:

1/7
(*Present age questions inheritance*) 1. The present age has questioned many things that mankind has inherited from his forefathers.
(*Produced questions*) 2. Thus the present age produces so many "contemporary issues" and "pressing social questions."
(*Many questions*) 3. Look at all the types of questions buzzing through the world today: the Social Question, the Women Question, the Education and School Questions, the Rights Question, the Hygiene Question etc., etc.
(*People's answers*) 4. People seek to answer these questions with the most varied means.
(*Many solutions*) 5. The number of people who emerge with every sort of remedy, in order to "solve" this and the other problems, or at least to contribute something to their solution, is immeasurably large.
(*Three philosophic answers*) 6. And every variety of human personality offers an answer: the radicals who conduct themselves with revolutionary fervor; the moderates who respect the already existing condition of things and seek to develop them into something new; and the conservatives, who immediately get upset when any aspect of the old institutions and traditions are attacked.
(*Every possible viewpoint*) 7. And in addition to these primary viewpoints every possible intermediate position appears.

12

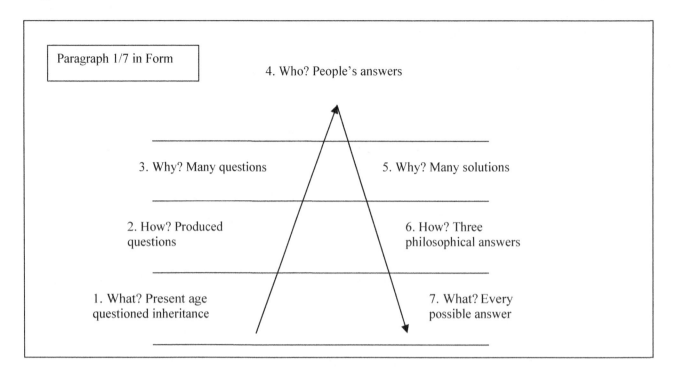

The polarities are clear with the first three sentences posing the questions and the final three giving the answers. The fourth sentence addresses the question "who?" quite nicely with the sentence "people seek to answer."

With these three examples and the study guide in the Appendix you can start reading the text and making notes. The method can be quickly put into practice and with time you will get really good at reading and making synopses. My synopses are *my own* attempt at understanding the form and content and should in no way serve as a standard for your own work. The next section contains my overview and synopses of the essay.

*   *   *

Mortimer Adler on how to read a book: Mortimer Adler once a graduate student at Columbia University noticed in a great books study group that there were two types of readers: naturally gifted and sloppy. Adler realizing that he was not a master reader spent his time noting the habits of superior readers. In his How to Read a Book, he outlined the habits and methods of reading great literature for a high level of mastery. The steps of a good reader are:

- know the type and purpose of the book (history, philosophy, or science);
- read the title and preface of the book to see the author's intent and thesis;
- read quickly through the whole book in order to get a feel for the content;
- read it again to see how and if the author accomplishes his task;
- and finally make synopses of each chapter and see how the parts fit into the whole.[1]

These steps can make a poor reader into a good one over time because Adler's suggestions expand the consciousness of the reader. The goal is to experience the book as an artistic whole, that is, to see the book in one glance and to know how the parts relate to the whole. Adler states unambiguously that few books qualify as great books and that a truly "great book" helps the reader to frame and navigate the essential questions of life.

---

[1] Adler's first edition of How to Read a Book is more exciting to read than the later republished edition now available. I used his method in the study of several great books with much success. Plato's Republic consisting of ten chapters is a masterpiece of form and content: the first 5 chapters tackles the state and society and chapters 6-10 the path of the Philosopher King. Chapter 1 asks the questions what about the afterlife and justice and chapter 10 gives the answer in reincarnation. Without Adler, I would have been bogged down in facts and arguments of the book and thanks to him I learned to 'see' the whole book at once.

One reads a great work in its entirety, and reconstructs the book section for section until the whole is understood in the parts and the parts in the whole. Only then can one conclude whether one agrees with the author's method or comprehends the higher meaning of the book. There is no greater satisfaction in reading than coming into an intimate understanding with an author of a book.

In reading Rudolf Steiner's work the first question to ask, according to Adler, is about the purpose and intent of the author. Steiner states in the beginning of his essay that his intention is to tell about the inner nature of the human being and education in light of spiritual knowledge. However, his organic-spiritual writing style is only mentioned in the prefaces and forewords of his main works such as The Philosophy of Spiritual Activity and Theosophy.[2] One would indeed need a broader knowledge of Steiner's 29 books and 5,000 lectures in order to discover the totality of his intent. For now let us be content with Steiner's goal of an organic style which the readers must eventually test for themselves.

Seeing in Wholes: What does it mean to see in wholes? It means to see things in a picture. What value is there in seeing in pictures? Diagrams and pictures allow us to survey, compare, and contrast different aspects of a whole.

The new consciousness requires that we be trained in thinking and seeing in wholes. Pure logical everyday thinking avoids thinking in wholes. Logical thinking reaches conclusions by synthesizing unrelated elements into a forced whole (typical psychologists studying mass human behavior), or analyzes wholes into fragmented parts (typical biologist studying living processes). We can move beyond logical thinking.

Seeing in wholes will, in the future, be a large aspect of educational practice. Someday educators will be teaching out of this tableau consciousness. Steiner gave many suggestions on how to teach seeing in wholes to children: in teaching about plants, present the plant connected to the environs in a picture relating the sky, earth, weather, and sun to the plant's existence; in teaching history always give an overview from the beginning of civilization to the topic at hand so that the themes find their meaning in a context of a whole. Waldorf offers countless examples.

Now, for adults the ultimate goal is to learn to see in wholes particularly in the realm of ideas. Steiner believed an active consciousness or seeing in wholes would lead the individual to a state in which she became the master of ideas. The most coercive addiction does not come from nicotine, but from our rigid thought patterns. Through systematic and regular study of ideas in an artistic way, we begin to gradually take control of our consciousness. The power of seeing one's own life as a whole, reported by those who had a near-death- experience, has a transformative power on the course of one's life.[3] A Primer for Spiritually Thinking Educators can become a practice guide for teachers for seeing in wholes just as Steiner had intended it to be.

The Musical Nature of Organic Thinking: Beyond seeing in wholes is seeing in levels. When angels think they move through a series of perspectives. They are not limited by time and space and therefore can see in wholes. It is said that spiritually enlightened individuals, when communicating higher truths, use a language based on this type of perspectives-thinking. George Ritchie, the author of Return from Tomorrow, recognized the same style of angelic thinking when he was out of his body, as when he completed an organic study of Steiner's Philosophy of Spiritual Activity, that is, when he was shown Steiner's organic style by F. Lowndes. Ritchie reports that in viewing his life all scenes took place at once as if all the scenes in a play took place at the same time.

In death, or out of the body, *we do not experience things sequentially but in simultaneous interweaving pictures*. The idea-pictures follow archetypes and patterns which are non-static. Musical analogies can be helpful, as music has to do with structures and motifs. A motif is repeated again and again with subtle changes, different tempos, and notes etc., clearly heard in Beethoven 5th symphony. Thinking can become musical, as it does in poetry and in some essays when there is a repetition of motif. Philosophy (or ideas in general) can be captured in a musical form in the sense that an idea can be presented in various levels, intervals, and perspectives.

Thinking need not be limited to isolated and unrelated thoughts arbitrarily strung together. An organic ordering of ideas brings us closer to this musical ideal. Music, like religion, can become ritual. The multiple-

---

[2] See Florin Lowndes' Das Erwecken des Herz-denkens, the Appendix of this essay, and A Study Guide to Rudolf Steiner's Heart-Thinking for a list of quotes from Steiner's books and lectures on his writing and thinking style. It is fair to say Steiner was never asked directly about his organic style.

[3] See George O'Neil's The Human Life. The book contains a "life chart" to be filled out. O'Neil was a pioneer in seeing in wholes and writing in organic forms. Rumor has it, he saw a whole chapter, and even the individual sentences, as a picture, and from this picture composed and wrote down the chapter.

perspectivism of organic thinking makes thinking into a ritual, or a ritualized thinking, which leaves our minds open for new intuitions.

Some Notes on the Primer for Spiritually Thinking Educators:

In the next chapter is the translation. I numbered the paragraphs, and the sentences for quick reference (the numbers in the fraction indicate paragraph count, then sentence count 1/7, 2/5 etc.). A series of hyphens in front of certain paragraphs has been given letters such as 15/a/12, 15/b/4 and these paragraphs should be treated as *parenthetical remarks* which belong to paragraph 15/4. After every paragraph there is a blank space for a short one- or two-sentence synopsis and a place for a catchword(s) representing the essence of the synopsis. At the end of each of the thirteen sections is a page where you enter your sentences and catchwords into diagram form. Once all sixty-five paragraphs of the text have been condensed, you can enter your sentences onto a large piece of paper so that you can view the whole. For a more in-depth understanding of the organic thinking process, of making synopses, and of the purpose of the wave-forms go to the Study Guide to Heart-thinking.

At the end of the <u>A Primer</u> ... are copies of my synopses and structuring of the text. I placed them there so you can have an idea of what a final copy could look like. I have attempted to simplify this work and text in order that the readers can jump in as quickly as possible. In the long run, Steiner's work will only make sense to those brave enough to wrestle with the being of organic thinking.

A Primer for Spiritually

Thinking Educators

A Primer for Spiritually Thinking Educators

1/7

1. The present age has questioned many things that mankind has inherited from his forefathers.

2. Thus the present age produces so many "contemporary issues" and "pressing social questions."

3. Look at all the types of questions buzzing through the world today: the Social Question, the Women Question, the Education and School Questions, the Rights Question, the Hygiene Question etc., etc.

4. People seek to answer these questions with the most varied means.

5. The number of people who emerge with every sort of remedy, in order to "solve" this and the other problems, or at least to contribute something to their solution, is immeasurably large.

6. And every variety of human personality offers an answer: the radicals who conduct themselves with revolutionary fervor; the moderates who respect the already existing condition of things and seek to develop them into something new; and the conservatives, who immediately get upset when any aspect of the old institutions and traditions are attacked.

7. And in addition to these primary viewpoints every possible intermediate position appears.

Synopsis:_____

_____

Catchword:_____

2/5

1. If one is able to have a deeper insight into life, one will not be able to avoid the feeling one gets from them [the political phenomenon].

2. It arises out of the fact that humanity is confronted by demands, and our age meets those demands with inadequate means.

3. Many individuals would like to reform life without knowing life in its true foundations.

4. If these individuals want to make suggestions about how something in the future should come about, they should not be satisfied with a superficial knowledge of life.

5. They must investigate life to its very depths.

Synopsis:_____

_____

Catchword:_____

3/5

1. Life in its entirety is like a plant, which not only contains that what the plant offers to the eye, but conceals, in addition, a future level of development in its hidden depths.

2. If an observer had a plant in front of him that just grew leaves, he understands very well that after some time flowers and fruit will be on the leaf-carrying stem.

3. Even at this stage, in hidden form, the plant contains the hereditary factors for the flowers and fruits.

4. How should an observer, however, be able to predict what these organs will look like, if he merely wants to investigate that aspect of the plant which is presently visible to the eye.

5. Only that person is able to do so, who has come to learn the true being of the plant.

Synopsis:_____

_____

Catchword:_____

4/8

1. Likewise, the human life contains in itself the predispositions of its future.

2. Yet in order to be able to say something about this future, one must penetrate the hidden nature of the human being.

3. Our era has, however, no real inclination to do this.

4. It busies itself with that aspect which appears on the surface and believes it is entering into realms of uncertainty when it attempts to delve into that which escapes external observation.

5. With plants, things are indeed much simpler.

6. The human being knows that other plants bear fruit again and again.

7. The human life is only present once; and the "flowers" which it should carry in the future have never been present.

8. Nevertheless, these future stages are in human beings, just as the flowers are present in the leaf stage of the plant.

Synopsis:_____

_____

Catchword:_____

5/2

1. Indeed, there is a possibility of saying something about a human life's future, if one penetrates below the surface of human nature to its true being.

2. All the varied reform ideas of the present age can only become truly fruitful and practical, if they are based on a deeper exploration of human life.

Synopsis:_____

_____

Catchword:_____

18

Enter the catchwords and synopses onto the diagram.

Ego, Yellow Level, who?

3.

Astral, Red Level, why?

2.   4.

Life, Green Level, how?

1.   5.

Physical, Blue Level, what?

6/5

1. Theosophy is obliged, as a consequence of its innate truth, to give a comprehensive, practical worldview concerning the nature of human life.
2. Whether what currently calls itself by this name is justified in making such a claim is not the point.
3. The point has much more to do with the intrinsic virtue of Theosophy, and, therefore what it is in a position to be according to its intrinsic virtue.
4. It should not be an abstract theory that quenches a simple thirst for knowledge, nor should it be a path for a few individuals who selfishly would like to have for themselves a higher stage of spiritual development.
5. It could be a co-worker in the most important of humanity's contemporary tasks for the development of humanity's well-being. 1)

Synopsis:_____

_____

Catchword:_____

7/3

1. Indeed, it will have to take into account the necessity of encountering quite a few attacks and reservations if it acknowledges such a mission.
2. Radicals, moderates, as well as conservatives, in all walks of life, will have to voice their doubts about Theosophy.
3. Because its foundation lies far beyond all political movements, it cannot please any party at the present time.

Synopsis:_____

Catchword:_____

8/9

1. This foundation has its roots solely in a true knowledge of life.
2. Individuals who understand life will be able to determine their tasks solely out of life itself.
3. They will not promote reckless programs; for they know that in the future no other fundamental laws of life can prevail other than those that prevail already in the present.
4. Thus, a respect for that which already exists necessarily suits Theosophy.
5. Though Theosophy may find in the existing institutions much that needs improvement, it will not fail to see in the existing institutions the seeds of the future.
6. In addition, it also takes into account that in all becoming there is growth and development.
7. Thus the seed of transformation and of growth in the present institutions will be apparent to Theosophy.
8. It does not invent programs; it reads them out of that which already exists.
9. However, what it reads in this way, becomes, in a certain sense, itself a program, for it has in fact the essence of development in it.

Synopsis:_____

_____

Catchword:_____

9/1

1. Exactly for this reason the Theosophical knowledge of the being of man must provide the most fruitful and practical means for the solution of the crucial questions of the present age.

Synopsis:_____

Catchword:_____

10/3

1. In this text this shall be demonstrated for such a question, namely the education question.

2. Neither programs nor demands will be advanced, but only the true nature of the child will be   described.

3. Out of the nature of the developing human being, the point of view for education will arise quite naturally.

Synopsis:_____

_____

Catchword:_____

Enter the catchwords
and synopses onto the
diagram.

Ego, Yellow Level,
who?

8.

Astral, Red Level,
why?

7.   9.

Life, Green Level,
how?

6.   10.

Physical, Blue Level,
what?

11/1

1. For if one desires to know the nature of the developing human being, then one must proceed, if at all, from a consideration of the hidden nature of the human being.

Synopsis:_____

Catchword:_____

12/4

1. What sensory observation comes to know about the human being and what the materialistic view of life wants to recognize as the only aspect of the being of man, is for spiritual research only one aspect, one member of human nature, namely his physical body.
2. This physical body is subject to the same laws of physical existence, it consists of the same material and forces as the entire, commonly so-called lifeless world.
3. Therefore, Theosophy says: the human being shares this physical body with the mineral kingdom.
4. And it considers only that part to be the physical body of man, which combines, connects, creates formations out of, and dissolves various minerals/materials in accordance with the very same laws, which are also at work in like substances in the mineral world.

Synopsis:_____

_____

Catchword:_____

13/4

1. Over and above the physical body, Theosophy recognizes yet a second member in man: the life body or ether body.
2. The physicist doesn't need to take issue with the term ether body.
3. "Ether" is defined here as something other than the hypothetical "ether" of physics.
4. One should understand the term as a characterization for what will be described in the following.

Synopsis:_____

Catchword:_____

14/9

1. In recent times, it was considered a totally unscientific proceeding, to discuss such a thing as an "ether body."
2. Towards the end of the 18th century and in the first half of the 19th century it was, however, not "unscientific."
3. For then one could claim that the material and forces, which are at work in a mineral, cannot transform the mineral into a living being on their own accord.
4. A special "force" must inhabit it, which one designates as the "life force."
5. One imagines, for example, that in a plant, in an animal, and in the human body such a force works and brings forth the vital signs, just as a magnetic force produces attraction.
6. In the era after the age of materialism such an idea has been discarded.
7. For one claims that a living being is constructed in the same manner as a so-called lifeless one; no other forces are present other than the mineral ones; they function only in a more complex manner; they build a more complicated picture.
8. Presently, only the most rigid materialists still continue to reject the existence of a "life force."
9. A whole line of scientific thinkers have taught that one must accept something like a life force or life principle.

Synopsis:_____

_____

Catchword:_____

15/4

1. In this way modern science has come close, in a certain sense, to what Theosophy claims about the life body.
2. Nevertheless, there is a significant difference between the two.
3. From the empirical facts of sense-observation, modern science arrived, on account of certain intellectual considerations, to the acceptance of a kind of a life force.
4. However, this is not the method of a true spiritual investigation, like the kind Theosophy adopts, and on the results of which it bases its statements.

Synopsis:_____

Catchword:_____

15/a/12

1. – It cannot be emphasized often enough how in this point Theosophy differs from the popular science of the present.
2. It considers the experience of the senses as the foundation of knowledge, and whatever cannot be placed on this foundation, it maintains, is not knowable.
3. It draws conclusions and deductions out of the impressions of the senses.
4. It rejects anything that goes beyond it, and says that it lies far beyond the limits of human comprehension.
5. For Theosophy, such an opinion equals that of a blind person, who would only allow to be valid what one can touch, and the inferences deduced from what was touched, and he rejects the statements of a non-blind person as beyond the human capacity for knowledge.
6. For Theosophy shows that the human being is capable of development, that he can conquer new worlds by unfolding new organs.
7. Just as color and light are around the blind, and they can't perceive them because they do not have the corresponding organs, so Theosophy says: there are many worlds around the human being, if he would only just train the necessary organs for this purpose.
8. Just as the blind look into a new world after they are operated on, so also can the human being know through the unfolding of higher organs totally different worlds than those which the normal senses allow him currently to perceive.
9. Now whether one who is physically blind can be operated on or not, that depends on the construction of his organs; all higher organs however, through which the human being can enter into higher worlds are in germinal form present in every human being.
10. Everyone can develop them who has the patience, stamina, and energy to apply those methods on himself, which are described in the journal "Lucifer-Gnosis" in the essays "How One Attains Knowledge of Higher Worlds?" 2)
11. Thus, Theosophy never says: human beings have limits to knowledge because of their organization; but says: there exist worlds for which human beings have the organs of perception.
12. It talks only about the means to expand beyond these temporary limitations.

15/b/4

1. – In addition it maintains the same view about the researching of the life or ether body and everything else, which is referred to in the following, as the higher bodies of human nature.
2. It acknowledges that only the physical body is accessible to investigation through the physical senses, and from this approach one can conclude, through deduction, the existence of a higher body.
3. But it shares how one can access a world in which those higher bodies of the human being appear to the observer, practically in the same way as the colors and light of the objects appear to the person born blind who has had corrective surgery.
4. For those who have developed their higher organs of perception, the ether or life body is an object of observation, not just an object of intellectual theorizing and deductions.

Enter the catchwords
and synopses onto the
diagram.

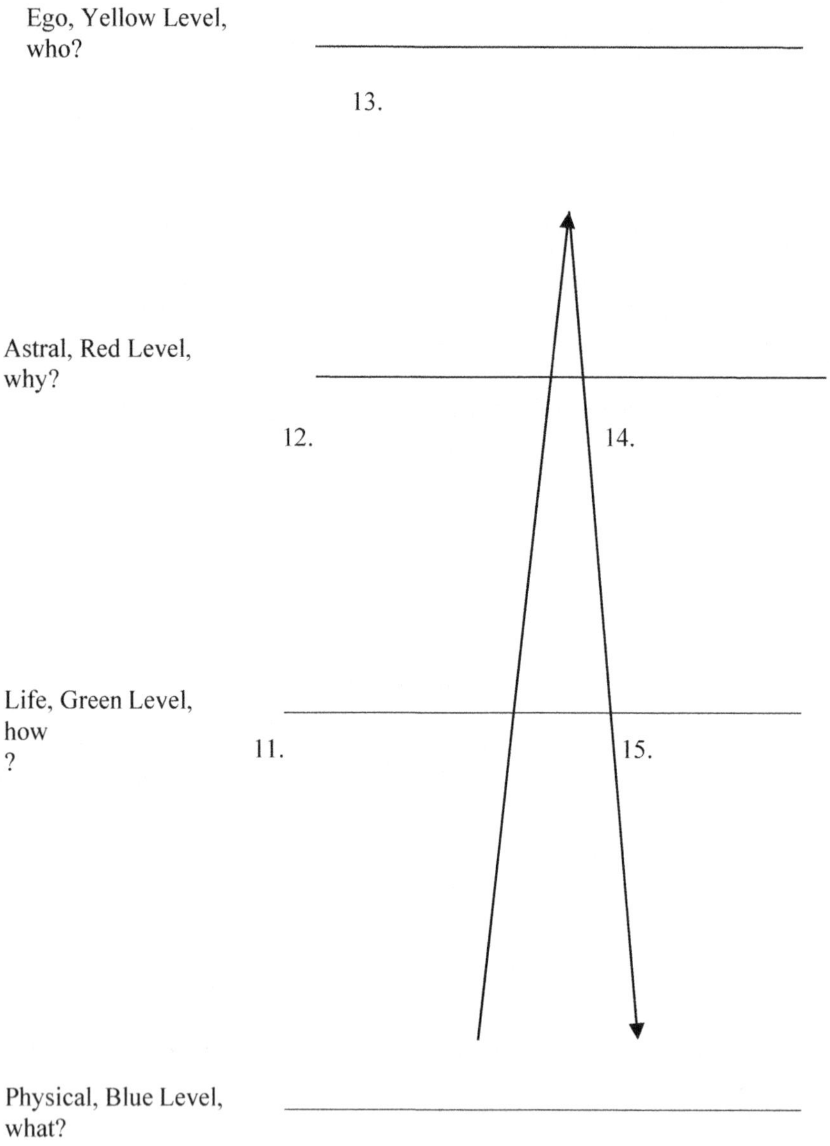

Ego, Yellow Level,
who?
_____

13.

Astral, Red Level,
why?
_____

12.   14.

Life, Green Level,
how
?
11.   15.

Physical, Blue Level,
what?
_____

16/6

1. The human being has this life body or ether body in common with plants and animals.

2. It causes the matter and forces of the physical body to enter into the phenomenon of growth, reproduction, and the inner movement of the vital fluids and so on.

3. It is thus the builder and sculptor of the physical body, its inhabitant and architect.

4. Therefore, one can also call the physical body a copy or expression of this life-body.

5. In reference to the size and shape both approximate one another but are in no way equal.

6. In animals and even more so in plants, the ether-body however differs considerably from the physical body in shape and expansion.

Synopsis:_____

_____

Catchword:_____

17/8

1. The third body of the human being is the so-called sentient or astral body.

2. It is the bearer of pain and pleasure, of drives and desires and passion etc.

3. A living being can possess none of these things, if it consists only of a physical body and ether body.

4. One could summarize all of the above-mentioned in the expression: feeling [Empfindung].

5. The plants have no feeling.

6. When in our times some scientists conclude that the plants have a certain ability for feeling from the fact that some plants answer stimulation with movement; they show thereby only that they do not know the essential nature of feeling.

7. The point is not whether this plant-being responds to an external stimulus, but the relevant point is whether the stimulus is reflected in an inner process such as pain or pleasure, drive, desire, and so on.

8. If one does not stick to this criterion, one would be justified in saying that the blue litmus paper has a feeling from particular substances, because it turns red during contact with them. 3)

Synopsis:_____

_____

Catchword:_____

18/2

1. The human being has a feeling body in common only with the animal kingdom.

2. It is the bearer of the feeling life.

Synopsis:_____

Catchword:_____

19/3

1. One should not fall into the same error of certain Theosophical circles and think the ether body and feeling body consist simply of finer materials, such as exist in the physical body.

2. That would mean categorizing these higher bodies of human nature into a materialistic framework.

3. The ether-body is an energy-formation; it consists of active forces not of material substances; and the astral or feeling body is a formation consisting of inwardly moving, colorful, luminous images. 4)

Synopsis:_____

Catchword:_____

20/3

1. The feeling body is different in form and size from the physical body.

2. It appears in humans in the form of an elongated egg in which the physical and the ether body are embedded.

3. It projects on all sides beyond the other two in a beautiful picture form.

Synopsis:_____

Catchword:_____

27

Enter the catchwords
and synopses onto the
diagram.

Ego, Yellow Level,
who?   _____

                    18.

Astral, Red Level,
why?   _____

         17.   19.

Life, Green Level,
how   _____
?
         16.   20.

Physical, Blue Level,   _____
what?

21/14

1. Now human beings have a fourth body in their constitution, which they do not have in common with other earthly creatures.
2. This is the bearer of the human "ego."
3. The little word "I" as is the case in the English language, is a name which differs from all other names.
4. Whoever reflects on the being of this name in the correct manner, they open themselves up to the path of knowing the true nature of the human being.
5. One can apply all other names equally to the correspondingly named object.
6. Anyone can call a table "table," a chair "chair."
7. With the name "I" this is not the case.
8. It cannot be used for designating another person; one can only call herself "I."
9. The name "I" can never sound in my ear except as a designation for myself.
10. In so far as the human being designates himself as "I," he must name himself within himself.
11. A being that can utter "I" to himself is a world unto himself.
12. Those religions, which are founded on Theosophy, have always felt this.
13. They said therefore: With the "I," the "God," who manifests himself to lower beings only externally in the phenomena of the surrounding world, begins to speak internally.
14. The bearer of the capacity described here is the "ego body," the fourth member of the human being. 5)

Synopsis:_____

_____

Catchword:_____

22/11

1. This "ego body" is the bearer of the higher soul of the human being.
2. Because of it, the human being is the crown of all creation.
3. The "I" is, however, in modern humanity, in no way a simple being.
4. One can know its essence, if one compares human beings in different stages of development.
5. One sees the uneducated savage and the average European, and compares these again with a highly developed idealist.
6. They all have the ability to say to themselves "I"; the "ego body" is present in all of them.
7. The uneducated savage however, follows with his "I" his desires, drives, and needs practically like an animal.
8. The more developed person says to himself concerning certain inclinations and desires: one may pursue this desire, but one holds back on others and suppresses them.
9. In addition to his original tendencies and passions the idealist has developed higher ones.
10. This whole process takes place as the "I" works on the other bodies of the human being.
11. Therefore, exactly in this process lies the task of the "I" that it ennobles and purifies the other bodies out of its own power.

Synopsis:_____

_____

Catchword:_____

23/10

1. Thus, in those human beings who have reached beyond the condition where the external world first placed them, the lower members are changed more or less under the influence of the "I."
2. In the level of development, in which the human being has just lifted himself above the animals, and in which his "I" lights up, he still resembles an animal with regard to his lower bodies.
3. His ether or life body is merely the bearer of the living forces of form, growth and reproduction.

4. His sentient body expresses only the kind of drives, desires and passions which are stimulated by the external, natural surroundings.
5. As human beings work their way up from this level of education, through consecutive lives or incarnations, to ever higher levels of development, his "I" transforms the other bodies.
6. In this manner the sentient-body becomes the bearer of purified feelings of pleasure and pain, refined wishes and desires.
7. And also, the ether or life body transforms itself.
8. It becomes the bearer of the habits, of permanent personal inclinations, of temperaments and memory.
9. A human being, whose "I" has not yet worked on his life-body, has no memory of the experiences which he faced.
10. He lives his life in the way nature implanted it into him.

Synopsis:_____

_____

Catchword:_____

24/3
1. The whole of cultural evolution can be understood in terms of the transformation of the lower bodies by the "I."
2. This work penetrates even into the physical-body.
3. Under the influence of the "I," the physiognomy changes, the gestures and movements change, even the whole appearance of the physical body is altered.

Synopsis:_____

Catchword:_____

25/6
1. One can also differentiate how the various cultural and educational means affect differently the particular bodies of the human being.
2. The ordinary cultural factors affect the sentient body; they instruct it in new kinds of pleasure and pain, and drives etc., compared with the ones it had originally.
3. Immersion in works of art affects the ether body.
4. Because the human being through works of art receives a notion of something higher and nobler than what the external environment offers, he transforms his ether body.
5. A powerful means for purification and ennoblement of the ether body is religion.
6. Religious impulses have in this way their greatest mission in the development of humanity.

Synopsis:_____

_____

Catchword:_____

30

Enter the catchwords
and synopses onto the
diagram.

Ego, Yellow Level,
who?   _____

                         23.

Astral, Red Level,
why?   _____

            22.   24.

Life, Green Level,
how
?   _____
            21.   25.

Physical, Blue Level,   _____
what?

26/2

1. What one calls conscience, is nothing other than the result of the work of the "I" on the ether body by way of a series of incarnations.

2. When the human being realizes that he should not do this or the other thing and when through this realization a strong impression is made upon him, which is so strong it reaches all the way into his ether body, in this manner his conscience arises.

Synopsis:_____

Catchword:_____

27/4

1. Now this transformative work of the "I" on the lower bodies can be either of such a kind that it pertains to the whole of the human race, or it can be a completely individual achievement of one singular "I" on itself.

2. In the first transformation of the human being, the whole of the human species participates to a certain extent; the other transformation has to do with the individual's activity of the "I."

3. Now if the "I" becomes so powerful that it transforms the sentient body through its own strength, then one calls that which the "I" creates in this manner out of the sentient or astral body: spirit-self (or with the eastern expression: Manas).

4. Essentially this transformation has to do with an education and enrichment of the inner being by way of higher ideas and views.

Synopsis:_____

Catchword:_____

27/a/5

1. It is possible that the "I" attains an even higher most intimate transformation of the inner being of man.

2. This happens not only if the astral body is enriched but also if the ether or life body is transformed.

3. The human being learns many things in life and if one looks back from a certain point at one's life one can say to oneself "I have learned much," however, to a much lesser extent he will be able to claim during life a significant change of temperament of character, or about any improvement or deterioration of the memory.

4. Learning is connected with the astral body; the latter transformations, however, are connected with ether or life body.

5. It is for this reason that it is not an incorrect picture, when one compares the transformation of the astral body during life with progress of the minute hand of the clock and the transformation of the life body with the movement of the hour hand.

28/3

1. If the human being begins a higher or so-called occult schooling, then the important thing is, above all, that he takes on the latter transformation out of the inherent power of the "I."

2. He must work absolutely consciously and individually on transforming habits, temperaments, character, memory, etc.

3. The more he works on the life-body in this manner, the more he transforms it into life-spirit (the eastern expression, Budhi) in the sense of the Theosophical expression.

Synopsis:_____

Catchword:_____

29/2

1. At an even higher level, the human being succeeds in attaining the strength with which he can effect the physical body in a transforming manner (e.g., transforms blood circulation, pulse).

2. That which is transformed of the physical-body in this way is called the spirit-man (oriental terminology, Atman).

Synopsis:_____

Catchword:_____

30/5

1. The transformations - which the human being completes in his lower bodies as a member of the human species or as a part of a people, tribe, or family - have the following names in Theosophy.

2. The astral or sentient body transformed [by the "I"] is called the sentient soul, the transformed ether body is called intellectual-feeling soul, and the transformed physical body is called the consciousness soul.

3. One should not, however, imagine that the transformation of these three members is sequential.

4. It takes place in all three bodies at the same time from the moment the "I" lights up.

5. Indeed, the work of the "I" does not at all become clearly noticeable to the human being until a part of the consciousness soul has been formed.

Synopsis:_____

_____

Catchword:_____

Enter the catchwords
and synopses onto the
diagram.

Ego, Yellow Level,
who?

28.

Astral, Red Level,
why?

27.   29.

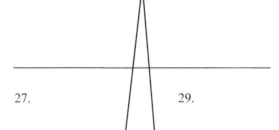

Life, Green Level,
how
?

26.   30.

Physical, Blue Level,
what?

31/1

1. One sees from what was just said that one can speak about the human being in terms of the four bodies of his nature: the physical body, the ether or life body, the astral or sentient body, and the I body.

Synopsis:_____

Catchword:_____

31/a/2

1. –The sentient soul, rational-feeling soul, consciousness soul, and also the higher bodies of the human being: spirit-self, spirit-life, spirit-man all occur as the result of the transformation of these four bodies.
2. If the topic of discussion is what carries and bears the characteristics of man, then in fact only these four bodies come into consideration.

32/5

1. As an educator, one works on these four bodies of the human being.
2. If one wants to work in the right way, one must then research the nature of these parts of the human being.
3. Now, one should never picture to oneself that these parts of man develop themselves in such a way that they would be at the same level in some point in life, for example, at birth.
4. Their development takes place instead in various life periods in various forms.
5. And the correct foundation for education and also for teaching is based upon the knowledge of these laws of the development of human nature.

Synopsis:_____

_____

Catchword:_____

33/7

1. Before physical birth, the growing human being is enclosed on all sides by a foreign body.
2. He does not enter into contact with the outer physical world on his own.
3. The physical body of the mother is his environment.
4. Only this body can work on the maturing human being.
5. The physical birth consists of exactly this process, that the mother's physical protective sheath frees and releases the human being, and thereby the environment of the physical world can work directly on him.
6. The senses open up to the outer world.
7. This takes over the influence on the human being, which the mother's physical protective sheath had previously provided.
Synopsis:_____

_____

Catchword:_____

34/5

1. For a spiritual worldview as it is represented in Theosophy only the physical body is born at this point, not yet the ether or life body.
2. As the human being is surrounded by the mother's physical protective sheath until the time of his birth, in the same way he is, until the time of the change of teeth - approximately until the seventh year of life - surrounded by an ether sheath and an astral sheath.
3. Only during the change of teeth, does the ether sheath release the ether body.

4. There still remains the astral sheath until the arrival of puberty. 6)
5. During this point in time the astral or sentient body also becomes free on all sides, just as the physical body at birth and the ether body during the change of teeth have been freed.

Synopsis:_____

_____

Catchword:_____

35/2
1. Thus Theosophy must speak of three births of the human being.
2. Until the change of teeth certain impressions, which should be intended for the ether body, can no more reach it than the light and the air of the physical world can reach the physical body as long as it is in the mother's womb.

Synopsis:_____

Catchword:_____

Enter the catchwords
and synopses onto the
diagram.

Ego, Yellow Level,
who?

33.

Astral, Red Level,
why?

32.   34.

Life, Green Level,
how
?
31.   35.

Physical, Blue Level,
what?

36/7

1. Before the change of teeth sets in, the free life body does not work on the human being.
2. Just as the physical body while in the mother's body receives forces which are not its own and within the mother's sheath it gradually develops its own, thus it is the case with the forces of growth until the change of teeth.
3. The ether body at first prepares its own forces in conjunction with the inherited foreign ones.
4. During the time of the freeing up of the ether body, the physical body is indeed already independent.
5. The freed-up ether body prepares what it has to give to the physical body.
6. And the culmination of this work is the appearance of the human being's own teeth that take the place of the inherited teeth.
7. They are the densest deposit in the physical body and accordingly appear last at the end of this period.

Synopsis:_____

_____

Catchword:_____

37/5

1. After this period of time the life body alone takes care of growth.
2. Yet this body still remains under the influence of the astral body and its enclosing sheath.
3. At the moment when the astral body becomes free, the ether body is finished with this developmental period.
4. This closing is sealed in puberty.
5. The organs of reproduction become independent because from this point on the freed-up astral body no longer works inwardly, but without its sheath it meets the outer world directly.

Synopsis:_____

_____

Catchword:_____

38/2

1. One cannot let the physical influences of the outer world work on unborn children, in the same way one should not let the forces work on the ether body before the change of teeth: these forces are the same to the ether body as the impressions of the physical surroundings to the physical body.
2. And in the astral body, it is only after puberty that one should let the appropriate influences come into play.

Synopsis:_____

Catchword:_____

39/8

1. No general phrases like "the harmonious education of all powers and talents" and similar expressions can be the foundation of a true art of education, but only upon a true knowledge of the human being can such an art be built.
2. By no means should it be asserted that the above-mentioned phrases are incorrect but that simply nothing can be achieved with them, just as nothing would be achieved by yelling at a machine; 'one must bring all its parts harmoniously in motion.'
3. Only one who doesn't only approach the machine with general phrases but with real knowledge of the machine in all its details can run it.
4. Thus, for the art of education, it is important to have a knowledge of the bodies of the human being and their development in detail ......

5. One must know which part of the human being one has to work on and how this work should be best conducted.

6. Indeed, there is no doubt that an art of education as it is indicated here can only gradually make headway.

7. This is due to the worldview of our times which will long into the future consider the facts of a spiritual world as the outflow of a mad fantasy, while its banal, completely unrealistic phrases will seem to be the result of a realistic way of thinking.

8. Here shall be described without any reservations facts taken by many to be a magical fantasy in the present age but that will be, however, accepted as obvious in the future.

Synopsis:_____

_____

Catchword:_____

40/9

1. With the physical birth, the physical body is pushed out into the physical surroundings of the outside world, while beforehand he was surrounded by the protective sheath of the mother.

2. What the forces and fluids of the mother's sheath provided for him at the earlier stage, the forces and elements of the outer physical world must provide for him now.

3. Until the change of teeth in the seventh year, the human body has a mission to complete that is essentially different from the missions of all other stages of life.

4. During this period the physical organs must bring themselves into certain forms; their structural proportions must maintain certain orientations and tendencies.

5. Later on growth takes place and this future growth happens on the basis of the forms that have developed themselves up until the time indicated above.

6. If the correct forms have taken shape, then correct forms grow; if malformations have developed themselves, then malformations grow.

7. One could not repair in the future what one as an educator has neglected in the time before the 7th year of life.

8. Just as before birth, nature produces the proper environment for the physical body of the human being, after birth the educator has to provide the correct physical environment.

9. Only this type of correct physical environment affects the child in such a way that his or her physical organs arrange themselves into the correct forms.

Synopsis:_____

_____

Catchword:_____

Enter the catchwords
and synopses onto the
diagram.

Ego, Yellow Level,
who?

38.

Astral, Red Level,
why?

37.   39.

Life, Green Level,
how
?   36.   40.

Physical, Blue Level,
what?

41/7

1. There are two magic words that describe how the child enters into a relationship with his environment.
2. These are: imitation and example.
3. The Greek Philosopher Aristotle called the human being the most imitative of all animals; for no other life period does this expression fit better than for the period of childhood before the change of teeth.
4. Whatever goes on in the physical environment, the child imitates it, and in the process of imitation his physical organs cast themselves into forms in which they remain.
5. One must understand the physical environment in the broadest imaginable sense.
6. To it belongs not only what takes place around the child in the material sense but everything else that happens in the environment of the child which can be perceived by his senses and can work out of the physical space upon his spiritual forces.
7. In addition belong all actions moral or amoral, informed and foolish which the child can see.

Synopsis:_____

_____

Catchword:_____

42/8

1. No moral clichés, no intellectualized instructions work on the child in the direction indicated here, but instead what the adults do in the child's environment visible to his eyes.
2. Instructions do not work in a formative manner on the physical body of the child but on the ether body; and the child is surrounded until the seventh year of life by the protective ether-sheath of the mother, just as the physical body is surrounded by the mother's physical sheath until birth.
3. What should develop in the ether body before the seventh year in terms of mental pictures, habits, memory etc. [are features] that must develop in a similar way "on their own," just as the eyes and ears develop in the mother's body without the effect of an external light source….
4. It is without a doubt correct what one reads in an excellent pedagogical book, in Jean Paul's Levanna or "Theory of Education": a world traveler learns more from his caretaker in the early years than in all of his trips around the world put together.
5. However, the child learns not through instructions but through imitation.
6. And his physical organs develop their form through the influence of the physical environment.
7. Healthy vision is developed when one brings the proper conditions, colors, and light into the child's environment; and the physical seeds of a healthy moral sense are forming in the brain and circulation, if the child sees moral actions in his environment.
8. If the child before his seventh year only sees foolish actions in his environment, then the brain takes on such forms which make him prone later in life to foolish acts.

Synopsis:_____

_____

Catchword:_____

43/18

1. Just as the hand muscles become strong and powerful when they do the work corresponding to their ability, thus will the brain and the other physical organs of the physical body of the human being be directed on the right track if they receive the correct impressions from their surroundings.
2. An example will illustrate best the topic at hand.
3. One can make a child a doll in which one folds together an old napkin turning two of the tips into arms, two into legs, and out of a knot, a head and then with some ink paint eyes and a nose and a mouth.
4. Or one could buy a so-called "beautiful" doll with real hair and painted cheeks and give it to the child.

5. It does not need to be discussed here that this doll is obviously something terrible and tends to ruin a healthy aesthetic sense for a lifetime.

6. The main question of education is quite another one.

7. If the child has in front of it a folded napkin, then it must out of its own fantasy fill in what is necessary to make it appear as a person.

8. This work of active fantasy shapes and forms the child's brain construction.

9. It develops just as the hand muscles develop when doing the corresponding work.

10. If the child gets the so-called "beautiful puppet" then the brain has nothing more to do.

11. It withers and dries up instead of developing....

12. If human beings could, like the spiritual scientist, look into the growing brain's forms, then they would without a doubt only give those toys which are appropriate for the organic stimulation of the formative activity of the brain.

13. All toys which consist of dead mathematical forms have a deadening and desolating effect on the formative forces of the child, while everything which affects them in the correct way stimulates a living imagination.

14. Our materialistic age produces few good toys.

15. What a healthy toy it is which through two movable pieces of wood represents two smiths who face one another and are hammering an object.

16. One can still buy such things in the countryside.

17. Also very good are those picture books in which figures can be pulled by stings from beneath, so that the child himself can turn a dead picture into an active one.

18. This creates inner stimulation in the organs, and as a result of this stimulation, the correct form of the physical organs is developed.

Synopsis:_____

_____

_____

Catchword:_____

44/2

1. These topics can only be touched on here; however, spiritual science will be called in the future to give detailed indications of what is necessary, and this much it is certainly able to do.

2. For spiritual science is not an empty abstraction but a sum of life-filled facts which can give guidelines for life's realities.

Synopsis:_____

Catchword:_____

45/10

1. Only a couple of examples might still be presented.

2. A so-called nervous, excitable child must be treated differently than a lethargic, unexcitable child as regards to his environment.

3. Everything comes into consideration from the colors of the room and the other objects, which normally surround the child, to the colors of the clothes, which one dresses him in.

4. One will often do the wrong thing if one doesn't let oneself be guided by spiritual science, for, in many cases, the materialistic view will seek the opposite of what is correct.

5. One must surround an over-excitable child with red or yellow-reddish colors and have clothes especially made in these colors; however it is recommended with the unexcitable child to chose something in blue or blue-grayish colors.

6. This process is based on the color, which will be stimulated in the inner soul-life as its opposite color.

7. Therefore, for example, red evokes its complement green; blue, an orange-yellow color; one can convince oneself of this fact if one stares for a while at the corresponding colored surface and then quickly direct ones eyes to a white surface.

8. The compliment is created by the physical organs of the child and affects the corresponding and necessary organ formation in the child.

9. If the excitable child has red in his surroundings, then it creates in his inner soul-life the complementary green.

10. And this activity of creating green affects the child in a calming manner; the organs take on the inclination of calming.

Synopsis:_____

_____

Catchword:_____

Enter the catchwords
and synopses onto the
diagram.

Ego, Yellow Level,
who?

43.

Astral, Red Level,
why?

42.   44.

Life, Green Level,
how
?

41.   45.

Physical, Blue Level,
what?

44

46/5

1. One thing must be thoroughly taken into account for this age group: namely that the physical body establishes its own measurement for what is wholesome.
2. It does this through the proper formation of desires.
3. One can say in general that the healthy physical body desires what is beneficial to it.
4. And as long as the main focus is the physical body of the growing human being, one should have an eye open for what healthy desire, drive, and happiness require.
5. Pleasure and desire are the forces which draw out the organ's physical forms in the proper manner.

Synopsis:_____

_____

Catchword:_____

47/5

1. One can commit a grave sin, regarding the above-mentioned topic, if one does not place the child in the correct physical relationship to its environment.
2. This can happen in particular to the child's food instinct.
3. One can overfeed the child in such a manner that it loses its healthy food instinct completely; whereas one can maintain the healthy instinct for the child by means of the proper nutrition, so that he desires everything that is healthy for him under the circumstances, even a glass of water, and rejects everything that causes him harm.
4. Concerning this question of nutrition, Spiritual Science will know what recommendations to give, even the details of nutrition and food, when Spiritual Science is asked to establish an art of education.
5. For Spiritual Science is a realistic offering for life, not a gray theory, as it can still appear today with certain Theosophists and their mistaken ideas.

Synopsis:_____

_____

Catchword:_____

48/3

1. Pleasure in and with their environment belongs to the forces that work on the physical organs in a formative manner.
2. That is, happy facial expressions of the educator, and above all, honest unforced love.
3. This type of love, which streams through and warms the physical environment, "hatches out" in the truest sense of the word, the forms of the physical organs.

Synopsis:_____

Catchword:_____

49/9

1. When the imitation of healthy individuals is available in an atmosphere permeated by love then the child is in his appropriate element.
2. Care should be given to exclude anything in the child's environment that the child should not imitate.
3. One should not do anything which afterwards one must tell the child "you may not do that…."
4. The strength of a child's inherent capacity to imitate can be recognized by observing how it paints and scribbles, thus imitating what it sees long before it understands what it is writing.
5. It is even a good thing if the child at first copies the alphabet and then learns its meaning.

6. For imitation belongs to the phase of development of the physical body, whereas understanding speaks to the ether body; and one should only work on this body after the second dentition, when his outer ether-sheath has fallen away from him.

7. In this age group in particular, the learning of all speech should especially take place through imitation.

8. The child learns speech best by listening.

9. All rules and artificial moralizing can have no positive effect.

Synopsis:_____

_____

Catchword:_____

50/4

1. In early childhood it is particularly important that such means of education as children's songs make a strong rhythmic and aesthetic impression on the children's senses.

2. Less value is to be placed on understanding the meaning; more value is to be placed on beautiful sounds.

3. The more refreshingly something works on the eye and ear, the better its practical value.

4. One should not underestimate what sort of organ-forming power is inherent, for example, in dancing movements accompanied by musical rhythm.

Synopsis:_____

Catchword:_____

Enter the catchwords
and synopses onto the
diagram.

Ego, Yellow Level,
who?

48.

Astral, Red Level,
why?

47.　　　　49.

Life, Green Level,
how
?

46.　　　　50.

Physical, Blue Level,
what?

51/33

1. The ether body sheds off the outer ether sheath with the arrival of the second dentition, and thereby begins a time in which one is able to educate the ether body from without.

2. One must be clear as to what can work on the ether body from without.

3. The transformation and growth of the ether body means the education, or better said, the development of inclinations, habits, conscience, character, memory, and temperaments.

4. One works on the ether body through pictures, through examples, and through a systematic directing of the imagination.

5. Individuals have to present themselves as living examples which the child will imitate until the seventh year of life; and further, between the change of teeth and puberty everything must be done in the environment of the growing human being so that his eyes awaken to spiritual content and meaning.

6. Meaning, which works through picture and parable, is now appropriate.

7. The ether body develops its power when a directed imagination can orient itself according to what it can decipher and use as a guiding principle from the living- or spirit-guided images and parables.

8. Neither abstract terminology nor the mere sensory works in the correct manner on the growing ether body, but 'the spiritually vivid' and living pictures do work.

9. Such spiritual vividness is the correct medium of education for this age group.

10. Thus, it is of primary concern that the young human being in this age has educators and personalities around him through which the desirable intellectual and moral forces can be awakened in him.

11. Just as the magic words of education are imitation and example during the first years of childhood, for the years which are in consideration here, they are: discipleship and authority.

12. A natural, uncoercive authority must represent a real spiritual worldview through which the young adult educates his conscience, habits, and inclinations, through which he brings his temperament into steadiness, and through whose eyes he sees the things of the world.

13. The beautiful poetic saying "every man must choose his own hero, in whose footsteps he labors up toward Olympus," is particularly valid for this age group.

14. Adoration and reverence are the forces through which the ether body grows in the correct manner.

15. And for whomever it was not possible, during the time period discussed here, to look up to someone with unlimited reverence and respect, he will face difficulties throughout his life.

16. Where that reverence is missing, the living forces of the ether body whither.

17. Let us picture the following in its effect on the young soul: an eight-year-old child is told about a highly regarded personality.

18. Everything he has heard about her fills him with awe.

19. The day nears when he can see this honorable personality for the first time.

20. He is overcome with tremblings of reverence, as he turns the door handle, behind which the honorable one will be seen....

21. Beautiful feelings, which such an experience can bring forth, belong to the lasting treasures of life.

22. And happy is that person who not only for a split second of life, but continually, is able to look up to his teachers and educators as naturally recognized authorities.

23. In addition to these living authorities, to these incarnations of moral and intellectual strength, must be added those authorities that are experienced spiritually.

24. The great examples from history, narrations of exemplary men and women must shape conscience, must shape the spiritual direction, not however in terms of very abstract moral maxims, which would only be able to have their proper effect when the astral body at puberty has lost its astral nurturing sheath.

25. One has to orient in particular the history classes in a direction that is shaped by such a point of view.

26. Before the change of teeth the stories, fairy tales and so on which one presents to the children, shall have happiness, refreshment, and gaiety as their only goal.

27. After this time, concerning the material that is narrated one must care that certain pictures of life come before the soul of the young human being that can be enthusiastically emulated.

28. Let us not forget the fact that bad habits can be cleared up through the correct didactic pictures.

29. In the main, admonishings help little against such bad habits and tendencies; however, if you let the living picture of a correspondingly bad person work on the youthful imagination and you show to what end a habit which comes into question leads, thus you can contribute much to its extinguishing.

30. Always remember that life-filled pictures in all their spiritual concreteness, not abstract ideas, effect the developing ether body.

31. Indeed, the aforementioned must be carried out with the greatest possible tact so that the thing does not have the opposite effect.

32. In telling stories, everything depends on the manner of telling it.

33. The oral telling of stories cannot be substituted by readings without further complications.

Synopsis:_____

_____

_____

_____

Catchword:_____

52/14

1. The content of spiritual-picturing, or as one could also call it, symbolic imagining, comes also into consideration in a different manner for the age between the second dentition and puberty.

2. It is necessary that the young human being learns the secrets of nature and the laws of life, not in intellectualized sober terminology, but in as much as possible in symbols.

3. Parables for conceptual connections must be brought to the soul in such a way that the laws of existence behind the parables are more intuited and felt rather than grasped in intellectual concepts.

4. "Everything passing is a parable," that must be the maxim guiding all education during these years.

5. It is eternally important for the human being that he receive the secrets of existence in parables, before they are brought before his soul in the form of natural laws etc.

6. An example may clarify this.

7. Let's imagine one wants to speak to a young person about the immortality of the soul, about its coming forth out of the body.

8. One should do it in such a way that one uses, for example, the illustration of the coming forth of the butterfly out of the chrysalis.

9. Just as the butterfly lifts itself out of the chrysalis, so after death the soul lifts itself out of its dwelling place in the body.

10. No person will grasp the actual process in intellectual concepts in the right manner, who has not first received them in such a picture.

11. Through such a parable one speaks not simply to the intellect, but to the feeling, the emotional life, to the whole soul.

12. Therefore, a young adult who experienced this approaches a subject in a totally different mood, then if the subject had been taught to him only later in intellectual concepts.

13. It is in fact truly terrible for the human being if he cannot, first, with his feeling life, approach the riddles of existence.

14. It is indeed necessary that parables are available to the educator for all scientific laws and world secrets.

Synopsis:_____

_____

Catchword:_____

53/20

1. One can see very clearly in the above-mentioned example, how fruitfully Spiritual Science must affect our practical life.

2. If someone, who constructs parables out of a materialistic, intellectualized manner of thinking, presents these parables to young adults, he will, as a rule, make little impression on them.
3. Such an individual must use all his intellectual capacities to contrive the parables in the first place.
4. Such parables that one has artificially constructed, unconvincingly effect the listeners with whom the parable was to be shared.
5. If one, however, speaks to another in pictures, then what works on that person is not simply what one has said or explained, but instead a fine spiritual stream flows, from the one telling it, to those individuals at the receiving end of the story.
6. If the storyteller himself doesn't possess the warm pious feeling toward his parables, then he will make no impression on him whom he is trying to reach.
7. In order to have the desired effect, one must believe in one's own parable as reality.
8. This one can only do if one has the spiritual scientific manner of thinking, and the parables are born out of Spiritual Science itself.
9. The true spiritual scientist need not torture himself with the above-mentioned parable about the soul arising out of the body, because it is, for him, the truth.
10. There is, for him, in the emerging forth of the butterfly out of the chrysalis on the lower level of the natural life forms the same process that on a higher level and in a higher form, repeats itself in the emerging of the soul from the body.
11. He believes this himself with all his might.
12. And this belief flows from the speaker to the listeners as a mysterious streaming and it enkindles conviction.
13. Pure life pours forth from the educator to the child.
14. However, this life requires that the educator creates out of the spring of Spiritual Science, and that his word and everything which is presented by him receives feeling, warmth, and color of feeling from a genuine spiritual scientific manner of thinking.
15. A glorious perspective presents itself thereby for the whole institution of education.
16. If this institution would let itself be fructified by the life source of Spiritual Science, then it would be itself full of life and understanding.
17. The groping so prevalent in this area would stop.
18. The entire art of education, of pedagogy, is barren and dead if it does not receive fresh energy again and again from this source.
19. Spiritual Science offers the corresponding parables for all world secrets, which are pictures taken from the essence of things, which were not first created by human beings, but were used by the powers of the world at its creation.
20. That is why Spiritual Science must be the life-filled foundation of all of the arts of education.

Synopsis:_____

_____

_____

Catchword:_____

54/5
1. Memory is a faculty of the soul upon which much value has been placed in this period of human development.
2. The development of the memory is connected to the reforming of the ether body.
3. Its education takes place in such a way that it becomes free during the time between the second dentition and puberty, and thus this also is a time period in which one must oversee consciously the future education of the memory.
4. The memory will have permanently less value than it could have for the human being, if in this period the correct methods are neglected.
5. The neglected human being cannot catch up later in life.

Synopsis:_____

Catchword:_____

55/12

1. A materialistic, intellectualized manner of thinking can make many a mistake in this domain.
2. An art of education, arising out of this manner of thinking, arrives quickly to certain prejudices against having knowledge simply acquired by memorization.
3. The materialists never tire themselves out when focusing all their cleverness against the pure training of the memory, and they utilize the most ingenious methods so that the child need not acquire anything by use of his memory that he does not first fully comprehend.
4. Goodness gracious, what is so important about understanding everything intellectually!
5. A materialistic, intellectualized thinking devotes itself so easily to the belief that there is no deeper understanding of the world other than in abstract concepts; and it will have difficulty arriving at an understanding that there are other forces of the soul that can be used to grasp the world, which are just as necessary as the intellect.
6. It is not meant solely as a figure of speech when one says that one can gain knowledge with feelings, with emotions, with the rational-feeling part of the soul, just as with the intellect.
7. Abstract concepts are only one medium of understanding the things of the world.
8. And they seem to the materialistic thinker as the only right one.
9. There are, of course, many individuals who do not believe themselves to be materialists and at the same time maintain that an conceptual understanding is the only manner of acquiring knowledge.
10. Such individuals proclaim an idealistic, perhaps even a spiritual, world conception.
11. However, in their souls they relate to the spiritual world conception in a materialistic manner.
12. For them, the intellect is once and for all the instrument of the soul for comprehending the material existence.
Synopsis:_____

Catchword:_____

Enter the catchwords
and synopses onto the
diagram.

Ego, Yellow Level,
who?

53.

Astral, Red Level,
why?

52.   54.

Life, Green Level,
how
?
51.   55.

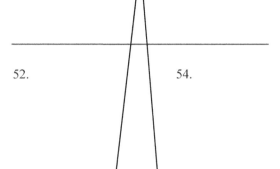
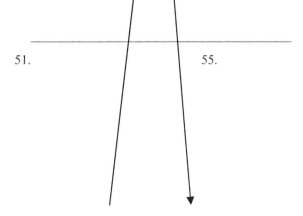

Physical, Blue Level,
what?

56/5

1. In reference to the profound foundations of human understanding, a section shall be presented here from the excellent book on education by Jean Paul.

2. The work contains golden insights about education and deserves much more consideration than it has had.

3. It is much more important for the educator than many of the established writings on this subject.

4. The section under consideration goes as follows: "fear nothing which is impossible to understand, even whole sentences; your expressions and your accent and enlightened drive to know makes intelligible the first half, and with this, and time, the other half too.

5. The accent is to children like with the Chinese and other people of the world, half of the language."

Synopsis:_____

_____

Catchword:_____

56/a/1

1. - "Consider how early they learn to understand their language so well, just as we understand Greek or another language before speaking it."

56/b/2

1. - "Trust the ability of time to unravel the connections and meanings.

2. A five-year old child understands the words "yet," "even," "of course," and "just"; try then to explain the meaning of the words not to the child but to the father!"

56/c/6

1. - Behind the tiny word "even" is a little philosopher.

2. When the eight-year old with his developed speech is understood by a three-year old, why then would you want to limit the child's speech with your baby talk.

3. Always speak a couple of years ahead (geniuses always speak to us a couple of hundred years ahead of us); with the one-year old speak as if he is two, with the two year-old as if he is six, for the difference in development diminishes in inverse ratio to age.

4. Consider, oh educator - you who give too much credit to the teacher for all learning- that the child has half of his world inherently in him, namely the spiritual one (for example, the moral and metaphysical intuition), and that's why language which is only equipped with physical imagery can't represent the nature of spiritual things, but can only point to them....

5. Pleasure and clarity in speaking with children should be given to us by way of their own pleasure and certainty.

6. One can learn from their language as well as teach them through language: intelligent and even correct construction of words, e.g. such as I have heard from three- and four-year old children: "a beerkeger," "bottler," and "caker" (for the profession of the same) – "the music violins" – "see how 1 o'clock it is" – etc."

57/19

1. True, this quote talks about understanding before intellectual understanding, in a different discipline from the one we are talking about here, however, the same holds true in what Jean Paul has said about language.

2. Just as the child learns the formation of the language in his soul without using the rules of syntax in intellectual concepts, so the young person must learn things in order to strengthen his memory, things which he will only really incorporate in an intellectual understanding later on.

3. In fact, one learns best to grasp things in concepts which one has acquired first in this life period through pure memory, just as one learns best the rules of a language which one already speaks.

4. The talk about memorization devoid of understanding is nothing other than a materialistic prejudice.

5. The young person needs, for example, to learn only the most elemental laws of multiplication using several examples, and no one needs an adding machine for this since the fingers are much better, and then he should learn his times tables through orderly memorization.

6. If one proceeds in this manner, one considers the nature of the developing individual.

7. One commits a grave sin if, during the time in which the education of the memory should be taking place, the intellect is called upon to do too much.

8. The intellect is a soul force which first appears in puberty, and as a result one should not try to influence it externally before this life period.

9. Until puberty the young child should acquire, through memorizing, the treasures which humanity has deliberated; then comes the time to penetrate with intellectual concepts what had earlier been thoroughly imprinted on the memory.

10. The human being should not therefore simply remember what he has learned, but he should understand the things he knows, that is, what he took into the depths of his memory, just as the child does with speech.

11. This holds true in a whole plethora of subjects.

12. First, learn historical events by pure memorizing, then understand the same in concepts.

13. First, imprint geographical themes on the memory.

14. Then understand the connections of the same, etc.

15. In a certain sense, all conceptual understanding should be taken out of the information stored in the memory.

16. The more the young adult already has in his memory before he proceeds to conceptual understanding, the better....

17. There is no need to emphasize the fact that these things apply only to the period of childhood that is discussed here, and are not for later on.

18. If one learns something later in life, then it can naturally be the case that the opposite method is correct and even more useful, although even here much might depend on the spiritual constitution of the person.

19. During the period of life we have discussed, one must not dry up the spirit by overfilling it with intellectual concepts.

Synopsis:_____

_____

_____

Catchword:_____

58/20

1. Also reflective of a materialistic way of thinking is a type of teaching that is based on pure sense-perception.

2. All perceiving and intuiting must be spiritualized for this age group.

3. One should not be satisfied, for example, when presenting a plant, seed, and flower solely in a way that is sense-perceptible.

4. Everything should become a parable of the spiritual.

5. A seed is not only what the eyes can see.

6. It has hidden in it an invisible new plant.

7. That such a thing is more than what the senses can perceive, this fact must be livingly grasped with emotion, feeling, and heart-warmed intellect.

8. They must divine through feeling, the secrets of existence.

9. One cannot object that through such a learning process that pure sense-perception is obscured: quite the contrary, by limiting oneself to pure sense-perception the truth remains stunted.

10. For the whole reality of a thing consists of Spirit and Material, and faithful observation need not be done with any less care, if one should bring the entire forces of the soul into effect, not only the physical senses.

11. If people could see all that is ruined in the Soul and Body as a result of a purely sense-perceptible approach to teaching in the way the spiritual scientist can, then they would not base so much of their teaching upon this method.

12. What is the benefit in the highest sense, when all possible mineral, plant, animal, and physical experiments are shown to young adults, if this is not done in conjunction with use of those physical parables to let them sense the spiritual mysteries.

13. A person with a materialistic view will surely not know where to begin with what was just discussed; although it is so obvious to the spiritual scientist.

14. However, it should also be clear to him that a truly practical art of education can never grow out of materialistic worldview.

15. As practical as the materialist believes himself to be, in reality he is really impractical when it comes to grasping life itself in a truly living manner.

16. The materialistic worldview seems fantasy-like when compared to the really real, while indeed the spiritual scientific worldview, which adheres to the facts of life, must necessarily seem fantastic to the materialist.

17. Without a doubt, many an obstacle will need to be overcome until the main ideas of Spiritual Science, thoroughly congruent to life itself, become incorporated into the art of education.

18. However, this is natural.

19. For in this time, its truths must still be strange for many people.

20. They will, however, be incorporated into the culture, if they are really the truth.

Synopsis:_____

_____

_____

Catchword:_____

59/2

1. Only through a clear consciousness of how the individual methods of education affect the younger people, can the educator always find the proper tact in order to arrive at the right solution for each individual case.

2. Thus one must know how the individual soul-forces, namely: thinking, feeling, and willing, are to be treated, so that their development reaches the ether body, while at the same time the ether body, between the second dentition and puberty, can form itself gradually to an ever more perfect degree through external influences,.

Synopsis:_____

Catchword:_____

60/8

1. During the first seven years of life the foundation is laid for the development of a healthy, powerful will by having a complete understanding of these educational principles.

2. For such a will must have its foundation in the fully developed forms of the physical body.

3. From the beginning of the second dentition, the main concern is that the now developed ether body gives to the physical body those forces through which its forms can grow and can become firm.

4. That which makes the strongest impression on the ether body also works in turn most strongly on the consolidation of the physical body.

5. The most powerful impulses will be called forth out of the ether body through the feelings and thoughts through which human beings consciously feel and experience their relationship to the eternal powers, that is, through religious experience.

6. Never shall the will of the human being (and his character) develop in a healthy manner, if he cannot experience deeply permeating religious impulses in this early cycle of life.

7. One sees, for example, in a unified organization of will, how the human being feels himself to be part of the whole world.

8. If the human being doesn't feel himself connected by strong threads to the divine-spiritual, then his will and character must remain unsteady, divided, and unhealthy.

Synopsis:_____

_____

Catchword:_____

Enter the catchwords
and synopses onto the
diagram.

Ego, Yellow Level,
who?

58.

Astral, Red Level,
why?

57.   59.

Life, Green Level,
how
?   56.   60.

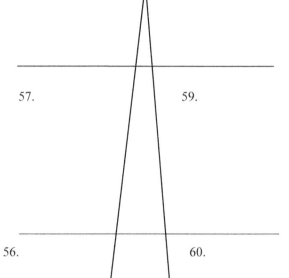

Physical, Blue Level,
what?

61/13

1. The world of feeling develops in the correct manner through the above mentioned parables and symbols, in particular through everything that is brought forth, out of history and other sources, of pictures of model human beings.

2. Also important for the formation of the realm of feeling is the immersion into the secrets and beauty of nature.

3. And particularly important to our consideration is the cultivation of a sense of beauty and the awakening of feelings for all things artistic.

4. The musical element must give to the etheric body the rhythm that allows the ether body to experience in all things the otherwise hidden rhythm.

5. Children who are denied the blessing of having their musical sense cultivated during these years will be the poorer because of it for the rest of their lives.

6. If this sense were totally lacking in him then certain aspects of the world's existence must remain hidden to him.

7. By the same token, the other arts should certainly not be neglected.

8. The awakening of a sense for architectural forms, for plastic forms, for sketching and drawing, for the harmony of colors, none of these should be left out of the educational plan.

9. No matter how Spartan life can be under certain circumstances, the objection can never be valid that the circumstances don't permit this type of activity.

10. One can achieve much with the simplest resources, if the educator has the proper attitude towards this activity.

11. Joy of life, a love of existence, energized for work, these traits develop for the whole of existence out of a cultivation of a sense of beauty and art.

12. And the relationship from human being to human being, oh how they will be ennobled and beautified through this sense.

13. Moral feeling, which is also cultivated during these years by way of good examples and model authorities, attains its certainty if through this sense for beauty the good is experienced as beautiful, the bad as ugly.

Synopsis:_____

_____

_____

Catchword:_____

62/4

1. Thinking in its essential form, as an inner life in abstract concepts, must still be kept at a distance during this period of childhood.

2. It must develop on its own time table, without outside influences, while the soul is receiving parables and pictures of life and the secrets of nature.

3. In this way thinking must develop in the midst of the other soul experiences between the seventh year of life and puberty, judgment must ripen in such a manner that after puberty arrives, the human being is capable of forming his own autonomous opinions about the subjects of life and of scholarship.

4. To the extent that one does not work directly on the development of the powers of judgment before this time, and, to the extent one indirectly influences them through the development of the other faculties of the soul, the better it is for all of the subsequent life of the individual concerned.

Synopsis:_____

_____

Catchword:_____

63/14

1. Spiritual Science delivers the true foundation not only for the spiritual aspect of education, but also for the physical.

2. At this juncture one might mention a characteristic example: gymnastics and children's games.

3. Just as love and joy must fill the environment of early childhood, therefore through physical exercises the developing ether body must experience a feeling of its own growth, of its continuously increasing power.

4. Gymnastic exercises, for example, must be done in such a way that in every movement, in every step, the feeling arises in the inner being of the young person: "I feel the growing strength within me."

5. And this feeling must make itself present in the inner being of the child in the form of a healthy instinct and pleasure.

6. In order to create such gymnastic exercises, one needs more than intellectualized anatomical and physiological knowledge of the human body.

7. For this task one needs a very intimate, intuitive knowledge based on a feeling awareness of how pleasure and contentment combine with postures and movements of the human body.

8. The creator of such exercises must be able to experience in himself how one movement, the positioning of the limbs, brings forth a pleasurable, comforting sense of strength, or the very opposite, of a loss of strength, etc....

9. In order to teach gymnastics and bodily exercises in this fashion, the educator requires, in addition, that which the spiritual scientific frame of mind can only offer.

10. One does not need to be able to look into the spiritual world itself; but requires only a sense for putting into practice in life that which arises out of Spiritual Science.

11. If spiritual scientific knowledge is put into practice, particularly in such practical affairs such as education, then the completely nonsensical discussions would cease as to whether this knowledge must first be proven.

12. He who employs it correctly, to him it would prove itself in life, through the fact that it makes one strong and healthy.

13. He would recognize this through the fact that it proves itself in praxis, that it is genuine, and that is why he will find a proof stronger through praxis than through any "logical" and so-called "scientific justification."

14. The spiritual truths one knows best in their fruits not through allegedly scientific advice, which can hardly be anything else but a logical cacophony.

Synopsis:_____

_____

_____

Catchword:_____

64/20

1. The astral body is first born in the age of puberty.

2. With its development, which is now open to the outside world, it will be possible to bring to the human being from outside all that can develop the abstract world of concepts, the power of judgment, and the free intellectual capacity.

3. It has already been mentioned that the soul capacities should develop first without intrusion but in harmony with the correct practice of the other means of education, just as the eyes and ears develop without outer influences in the womb.

4. Puberty comes at the time in which the human being is mature enough to form his own judgments about things which he had learned once before.

5. One could hardly more damage a human being than by awakening his own judgment prematurely.

6. For one can really only judge, if one has first memorized a topic to make judgments and comparisons about.

7. If one attempts such judgments before puberty, then the foundation shall be lacking for truly independent judgments.

8. All one sided-ness in life and all dreary creeds - which are based upon scraps of knowledge, and from these scraps of knowledge would like to challenge certain tried and true concepts of the collective human experience - originated from education mistakes in this direction.

58

9. In order to reach maturity in thinking, one must learn to have respect for what others have thought.

10. There can be no healthy thinking that has not been proceeded by a healthy feeling for the truth, a feeling which is supported by faith in authorities naturally accepted.

11. If one would follow this educational precept, one would not have to experience human beings who are too young declaring themselves mature enough to form judgments and thereby spoil their own power to receive without bias and from multiple perspectives the impressions of life.

12. Every judgment, which is not built on the necessary foundation of soul treasures, puts an obstacle in one's path in life.

13. Once one has formed a judgment about some thing, then one will always be influenced by it and one is not as perceptive of an event, as one would have been, had one not formed a judgment, which is in some way connected to this thing.

14. In young people the sensibility must live: first to learn then to judge.

15. What the intellect has to say about something should only be said when all of the other soul forces have spoken and before this time the intellect should only play the roll of intermediary.

16. It should only fulfill its role by understanding what has been seen and felt, and to take it in as it is without premature judgment coming and taking over.

17. Thus, the young person should be spared during this age of all sorts of theories about things, and instead emphasis should be placed on his meeting the experiences of life for the purpose of taking them into his soul.

18. One can certainly make known to the developing child those things that people have thought about this or that topic, however one should avoid that he engages in forming an opinion through premature judgment.

19. He should also be able to absorb opinions with his feeling, he should be able to hear without committing to the one or the other opinion and without taking sides: he has said this but the other something different.

20. It will require indeed, great tact in the development of such a sense in teachers and educators, but spiritual scientific sensibility is exactly in a position to offer this tact.

Synopsis:_____

_____

_____

Catchword:_____

65/12

1. Only certain aspects could be developed here concerning education and the spiritual scientific viewpoint.

2. Only limited guidelines were given here as to which cultural task this spiritual stream has to accomplish in this regard.

3. That it can accomplish such a task will depend on whether a sensibility for this way of thinking grows in ever wider circles.

4. In order for this to happen two things are necessary; first one has to give up one's prejudices against Spiritual Science.

5. He who really gives it a chance will see that it is not as crazy as many consider it to be today.

6. No accusation is made against them, for everything which our times offers in terms of methods of education must bring forth the opinion that spiritual scientists are crazy dreamers.

7. With such a superficial knowledge one could not form any other judgment, because there seems to be the biggest contradiction between Spiritual Science in the form of Theosophy and everything that modern education offers to people as a foundation for a healthy understanding of life.

8. Only a deeper knowledge uncovers how contradictory the modern views must remain without a foundation in spiritual science, and how these views require this foundation, and how they, in the long run, cannot survive without them.

9. Second, what is necessary depends on the healthy development of Theosophy itself.

10. Only if and when in Theosophical circles the knowledge will have penetrated that it depends on the teachers making it fruitful for the conditions of life in the most far reaching manner, and not just theorizing about them, then society will also consider Theosophy in a positive way.

11. Otherwise however, one will continue to think Theosophy is some kind of religious sect consisting of individual odd-ball enthusiasts.

12. If however, it achieves positive and useful spiritual work, then sympathetic recognition will not be denied the Theosophical Movement in the long run.

Synopsis:_____

_____

_____

Catchword:_____

60

Enter the catchwords
and synopses onto the
diagram.

Ego, Yellow Level,
who?

_____

63.

Astral, Red Level,
why?

62.   64.

Life, Green Level,
how
?

61.   65.

Physical, Blue Level,
what?

_____

Footnotes

Rudolf Steiner went through the trouble to create footnotes in organic form. Upon a close reading one notices that they make a nice organic six form. The two central footnotes (3 and 4) cover the discussion of sentience or feeling which in the organic scheme of things places them on the red or astral level. Footnotes 1 and 6 are on the physical level, 2 and 5 on the etheric level. Also note the inversion: footnotes 1, 2, and 3 discuss outer aspects of the topic, and the 4, 5, and 6 cover the results of spiritual vision.

1 This sentence should not be understood in the sense that Theosophy would only want to have something to do with the higher questions of life. It is true however that Theosophy is destined, in the sense mentioned above, to provide the foundation for the solution of *these* questions and it is just as true that Theosophy can be the source for every individual, regardless of where he stands in life, out of which he is able to draw answers for life's questions, as well as consolation, strength, certainty in life and in work. Theosophy can be the pillar for the greatest riddles of life as well as for the immediate fleeting needs even for the lowest order of possible situations of life.

2 One finds these essays in the books numbered 13-32 (and they will be continued in number 34) in the journal Lucifer- Gnosis.

3 One must refer to what is said here with particular clarity because particularly in our times there exists a great lack of clarity in this direction. Nowadays, many people gloss over the difference between plants and sentient beings, because they are not clear about the actual nature of *sentience.* If a being (or thing) responds in some way to an external stimulus it is not therefore justified to say that it has a sensation of the impression. It can only be said to have sensation if it *experiences* the impression in its *inner life*, that is if a sort of inner reflection of an outer stimuli is present. The great advances of natural science in our time, which the true Theosophist admires in the highest sense, have brought a lack of clarity in respect to higher concepts. Certain biologists don't know what sentience is; thus they ascribe sentience to even to non-sentient beings. What they, the biologists, believe 'sentience' to be, they allow themselves to ascribe such qualities to non-sentient beings. It is completely different from what spiritual science (Theosophy) understands as sentience.

4 One must distinguish between the *experiencing* of the sentient body *in himself* and the *perceiving* of the same by way of disciplined clairvoyance. What is meant by the above mentioned, is what lies before the opened spiritual eye.

5 One need not take offense at the term "ego body." It is not to imply something of a physical material nature. However, in spiritual science it is only possible to use the words of everyday language. And because they are applied normally to material objects, one must in using them in the theosophical sense first translate them into the spiritual sense of the word.

6 One would not understand the sentence above in its full clarity if one would make the objection that the child has memory before the change of teeth etc. and has, before the puberty, the capacities which are connected to the astral body. One must be very clear that the ether body, as well as the astral body, is present from the beginning, however, only within the already mentioned protective sheaths. These protective sheaths make it possible before the change of teeth, for example, to bring the memory into being in a very visible way through the ether body. However there are also, in fact, the physical eyes already present in the embryo while under the protective physical sheath of the mother. The outer physical sunlight should not be able to effect the development of the protected eye, in exactly the same sense external education should not shape the *education* of the memory before the change of teeth. We will come to see that the memory in this stage unfolds itself freely *by itself* if one gives it nourishment and doesn't see to its development through external educational measures. It is also the same before puberty with the characteristics - whose carrier is the astral body. One must give it nourishment, however always with the consciousness of the ideas mentioned above, since the astral body still lies under a protective sheath. It is one thing to take care of the seeds of development contained in the astral body *before* puberty; and quite another thing to place the self- sufficient astral body *after* sexual maturity into the outer world where he can work on the astral body *without* the sheath. This distinction is certainly subtle; however without going into the topic one can *not* understand the essence of education.

Synopses of the Thirteen Sections

I placed two lists of synopses as examples. When I first started doing this work, I had a difficult time making accurate synopses. In the example below, I tried to match the grammar and style with the levels. A 'what?' level synopsis will have a more static quality, a 'how?' synopses more action, and 'why?' synopsis more intention or feeling and so on. Unfortunately none of the diagrams in this booklet have color, so you will have to make your own and color them.

The physical level is blue; the life level is green; the astral level is red; and the ego level is yellow. When transferring your synopses and diagram onto new pieces of paper you can color each level and place the sentences onto the colored level. This way, one begins to associate the meaning with the color and form. I have placed all thirteen groups of five onto a large piece of art paper. A friend of mine prefers normal sheets of white paper and thus ends up with thirteen sheets of paper taped in 5-foot long ribbon strands. The curves themselves take on the colors of the levels too: the first curve is blue, second green, and third red and so on. Once one becomes familiar with the different levels and correspondences, one can become creative with the diagrams.

Some may wish to work on the individual paragraphs in order to study the thought-forms on the sentence level. The same type of diagram system works, even for paragraphs with thirty-three sentences. Working on the thought-forms at this level, the meditation and synopses are more detailed. My personal experience has been that the work at the sentence level lends itself better for the study and practice of organic thinking. There is no way to exhaust the variety of Steiner's organic thinking and one should keep in mind that Steiner has *three* different editions of this essay, each having a different paragraph count!

The Study Guide in the last section gives on overview of the organic forms and other variations. All of this requires time and study before the thought-forms become second nature. The Study Guide gives an important outline on how to run a study group. Synopses made by a group can be the most rewarding work.

1-5. what? The present age's reform movements require a deeper knowledge of human life.

6-10. how? Theosophy provides a knowledge and means to address problems in mainstream institutions.

11-15. why? Theosophical and scientific views are similar but methods differ concerning the life force and mineral world.

16-20. who? Steiner gives a picture of the shape and function of the astral and ether bodies.

21-25. why? The role of the ego body is to purify and ennoble the other bodies i.e., cultural evolution.

26-30. how? Over many incarnations the I forms the three souls and consciously works on the three spirits.

31-35. what? Education is based on the births of the 3 bodies and life periods.

36-40. how? The ether and astral bodies prepare themselves in seven year cycles and require the appropriate influences; educational example for ages 0-7.

41-45. why? The teacher educates the 1st seven years by providing the proper environment/adult behavior, clothing, toys.

46-50. who? The wisdom of the physical body: it desires naturally what is good for it such as certain foods. The teachers' love and pleasure in the environment, modeling exemplary behavior and speech, songs/dance, hatch out the children's organs.

51-55. why? Educating the ether body requires tact in teaching spiritual parables (laws of existence), uncoercive authority, feeling life of teacher, and memory training vs. materialistic prejudice against learning without conceptual understanding.

56-60. how?   Jean Paul says fear nothing that is impossible to understand: (Thinking) learn things,   again later with intellect, (Feeling) divine secrets of nature, and (Will) religious experience.

61-65. what?   The world of feeling is cultivated through art, joy of life and moral persons and the birth of the astral body requires learning to form judgments about what is learned. The future of spiritual science.

Synopses of the Sixty-five Paragraphs

1/7 What? The present age has many questions and many viewpoints from which they answer them.
2/5 How? The reformers address problems with means which are inadequate; reformers don't understand life. 3/5
Why? Life is like a plant and the observer must learn its hidden nature i.e., the hereditary factors.
4/8 How? Human life can be known by penetrating inner nature of the human being.
5/2 What? All reform ideas are fruitful if based on a deeper understanding of human life.

1-5. What? The present age's reform movements have inadequate means to reform life and such ideas require a deeper knowledge of human life.

6/5 What? Theosophy in spite of its reputation can be a co-worker in developing human well-being. 7/5
How? Theosophy's foundation will encounter critiques from all political parties.
8/9 Why? Individuals who understand life can work out of the seeds of existing institutions with the Theosophical program.
9/1 How? Theosophical knowledge provides a means for a solution to social questions.
10/3 What? This text gives a picture of the true nature of the child, and the point of view for education arises quite naturally.

6-10. How? Theosophy provides a knowledge and means to address problems in mainstream institutions.

11/1 What? If one desires to know the developing human being, then one must proceed from its hidden nature. 12/4
How? A materialistic view recognizes the physical body; Theosophy says the physical body operates out of laws of the mineral world.
13/4 Why? Theosophy recognizes an etheric body above the physical body.
14/9 How? It is unscientific to discuss the ether body, even though a life force was accepted in science.
15/4 What? Modern science thru empiricism accepts a life force unlike theosophical-supersensible investigation.

11-15. Why? Start with the hidden nature: Theosophical and scientific views about the life force and mineral world.

16/6 What? The shape, size, and function of the ether body in the 3 kingdoms. 17/8
How? The sentient body's function in man is feeling; plants don't have one. 18/2
Why? The human being has it in common with the animals.
19/3 How? Modern Theosophical circles make materialistic mistakes by thinking that higher bodies have substances.
20/3 What? The shape and size of the astral body resemble an elongated egg in which physical and etheric bodies are embedded.

16-20. Who? Steiner describes the shape and function of the astral and ether bodies.

21/14 What? Human beings have a unique body, a unique name "I" or Ego Body.
22/11 How? The I makes man the crown of creation; there are 3 levels of ego development based on the I's purification of the other bodies.
23/10 Why? The I reworks the ether and astral bodies over the course of incarnations: by developing refined wishes, memory and inclinations.
24/3 How? Cultural evolution is the "I"'s transformation of the bodies; even the physical is changed.
25/6 What? Every day cultural life educates affect and taste; religion and art educate the ether body.

21-25. Why? The role of the ego body in transforming the other bodies i.e., cultural evolution.

26/2 What? Conscience is the "I" work on the ether body over a series of incarnations.

27/4 How? The group and individuals transform through the "I" – power, by enriching the self with higher ideas the sentient body and, thereby, create the spirit self.

28/3 Why? Through an occult schooling one must work consciously on transforming habits, temperaments, character, and memory and then thereby create the life spirit.

29/2 How? If the human being begins a higher schooling, then he has the strength to effect the physical body (blood circulation) and create the spirit man.

30/5 What? Transformations completed in a group are the formation of the sentient, rational-feeling, and consciousness souls by the "I"; the "I" is not visible until the consciousness soul is formed.

26-30. How? The "I"'s task is to create the three souls and the three spirits.

31/1 What? One can speak of the human being as having 4 bodies.   32/5
How? The educator works on the 4 bodies in life laws and periods.

33/7 Why? The child is enclosed in the mother's sheath and at birth frees from the protective sheath where it receives the influence of the outer world.

34/5 How? For Theosophy, the physical body at this point is born, not the ether; the change of teeth releases the ether, puberty releases the astral body.

35/2 What? Thus 3 births of the human being, and know that the impressions intended for the ether body cannot reach it until age seven, just as light can't reach the physical body in the womb.

31-35. What? Education is based on the births of the 4 bodies and life periods.

36/7 What? The ether body prepares with its own forces the inherited ones once it is freed at the change of teeth. 37/5
How? The life body takes care of the growth alone and is enclosed by the astral body; after puberty the astral works outwardly.

38/2 Why? The appropriate influences after the appropriate bodies are born. 39/8
How? Not phrases but real knowledge of the bodies will be described here.

40/9 What? Correct environment and organ formation are necessary task for ages 0-7.

36-40. How? Ether body prepares and takes over; the appropriate influences for the bodies; example of ages 0-7.

41/7 What? There are two magic words for age 0-7: imitation and example; e.g., all adult actions in the child's environment educate.

42/8 How? Clichés and instructions don't work on the child but what the child sees in adult actions; Jean Paul on early childhood.

43/18 Why? Brains and organs will be on the right track if one uses napkin dolls, pieces of wood and pop-up books for building imagination.

44/2 How? In the future spiritual science will give more indications.

45/10 What? And some more examples: dress the children who are excitable, nervous, with different colors.

41-45. Why? Educating the 1st seven years by providing the proper environment/adult behavior, clothing, toys etc.

46/5 What? The physical body has its own measurements of desire and it desires what is good for it naturally. 47/5
How? One could commit a grave sin by overfeeding instead of maintaining a healthy instinct for food.

48/3 Why? Pleasure in the environment - sincere happy facial expression – works on the organ formation and the teacher's love hatches children's organs.

49/9 How? One must exclude everything that is not to be imitated, learning thru understanding comes later just as we learn to write before understanding the letters.

50/4 What? Singing and rhythm, beautiful sounds, and dancing are organ forming.

46-50. Who? Physical body is maintained through pleasure in the environment: happy teachers, learning before understanding, singing, dancing.

66

51/33 What? What works on the ether body from without: eyes awakened by parables, vivid pictures, uncoercive authority, reverence, noble people in life and history, tact in teaching spiritual pictures.
52/14 How? The laws of existence and science must be intuited from parables not in intellectual concepts.
53/20 Why? Spiritual science provides storytelling and education with the proper life and feeling for the parables.
54/5 How? Memory is the reforming of the ether body and can't be neglected in this period.
55/12 What? It is a materialistic mistake to be against memory training and in favor of intellectual comprehension.

51-55. Why? Educating the ether body through parables, authority, feeling life of teacher, and memory training.

56/5 What? Jean Paul writes "fear nothing which is impossible to understand, expression makes language intelligible, the child is a philosopher."
57/19 How? Jean Paul's idea holds good: learn things first and then again in puberty in a conceptual manner: math, history; for elders the opposite works better.
58/20 Why? Not sense perception but parables are used to divine nature's secrets with feeling; sense perceptual methods ruin learning.
59/2 How? The educator can arrive at a clear idea of the methods and tact for all individual children: by knowing how thinking, feeling, willing are treated in the development of the ether body.
60/8 What? A strong will shall have its foundation in a fully developed physical body. That which works on the ether body strongly also works on the physical body such as religious experience which gives the feel of the strong threads of the divine.

56-60. How? Jean Paul says fear nothing that is impossible to understand: (Th) learn things, later with intellect, (Feel) divine secrets of nature, and (Will) religious experience.

61/13 What? The world of feeling is developed through pictures and parables, beauty of nature, feel for the artistic, musical sense, joy of life, love of existence come from a cultivated sense of beauty and art. Moral feeling is cultivated through model authorities.
62/4 How? Thinking in abstract concepts must be kept at distance and only after puberty should judgments be made.
63/14 Why? Spiritual science gives true foundation for physical education: children feeling their power forms the ether body, muscle testing. It will prove itself through the practice.
64/20 How? The astral body is born in puberty and then the student can judge what was memorized also respect first what others have thought, absorb opinions with their feelings.
65/12 What? These are limited guidelines for spiritual science's task; prejudice and the future of spiritual science if the work is positive.

61-65. What? World of feeling as cultivated through art, joy of life and moral persons. The birth of the astral body and learning to form judgments about what is learned. The future of spiritual science.

On the next two pages are very Spartan examples of how I filled in the thought-forms. In the first diagram I entered paragraph synopses for each paragraph and in the second catchwords for each sentence of each paragraph. The second example could have been done with more care and color. The essence I think is clear however. The goal is to see every aspect of all the thought forms. (Paragraphs consisting of twenty or more sentences will most definitely need a whole separate sheet of paper.)

Enter the catchwords
and synopses onto the
diagram.

Ego, Yellow Level,
who?

8. Because Theosophy respects existing institutions, it can transform them. It reads the seeds of the future!

Astral, Red Level,
why?

Theosophy's mission will be criticized by various political parties.

9. Theosophy's knowledge of man provides practical solutions for today's questions.

Life, Green Level,
how?

6.

Theosophy's world view could be a co-worker for human development not just a theory.

10.

This text answers the education question by deserving the child's true nature.

Physical, Blue Level,
what?

Paragraph Synopses 6-10.

Catchword Diagram

> Enter the catchwords and synopses onto the diagram.

Ego, Yellow Level, who?

8/4. Respect   5. Seed of Future   6. Growth

3. Not reckless   7. Present institutions

2. task for life   8. Reads program

1. Foundation   4. Method=program

Astral, Red Level, why?

7/3   9/1

3. Theosophy bey Politics

2. All views doubt theos.

1. Attacks on theosophy   1. Theos:Knowledge → fruitful means

Life, Green Level, how?

6/5   10/3

3. Intrinsic Value   3. Point of view Educ.

2. Justified?   4. Not abstract   2 Description of true child

1. Theosophy   5 Co-worker   1. Education/Question

Physical, Blue Level, what?

The Study Guide

The Study Guide to Steiner's Heart-Thinking

This section describes Rudolf Steiner's organic writing style called heart-thinking. A Steiner text requires an *organic* reading and study, before its power and truth can be accessed. The goal of this manual is to provide an outline for this new type of study. The readers will be introduced to an organic method of reading Steiner's work. The starter texts include the *Preface to the Revised 1918 Edition* and the *Second Appendix* to the Philosophy of Spiritual Activity.[4] These texts contain the nine main thought-scales of Steiner's organic heart-thinking. The readers can learn and enhance their work with these thought-forms and within a short amount of time start employing them into their own life.

Steiner wanted this method of heart-thinking to enhance people's experience of life. By learning to think organically we can see the world and one another differently. As our set of dynamic concepts increases, so does our ability to love. In a certain sense the wave-forms contained in these texts can only be cognized and activated by our heart-chakra. Group study of these texts will awaken a warm and harmonizing bond between members.

Much of Steiner's suggestions for spiritual development have not been systematically taken up by spiritual teachers and put into a form that is proven safe. The same goes for his heart-thinking. There is a concern that individuals through systematic practice of the suggestions given here can open their spiritual eyes. The physical, soul, and spiritual hygiene of the average person is lacking in today's society and therefore it is not, at this point in time, recommended to do the exercises in the essay *with the conscious intention of opening up higher faculties*. But, please, have fun working the thought exercises with the goal of increasing your sense of organic form and group camaraderie.

I. The Models

Rudolf Steiner never gave a clear statement of what his heart-thinking was and how to practice it. This fact has brought about much confusion, and most of Steiner's 'official' scholars[*] and publishers do *not believe* that his writing style has any organic method or model at all. I believe that there are many different kinds of heart- thinking. The one developed here, is a particular organizing principle called 'heart-thinking' by Rudolf Steiner.[5]

The models given here serve as suggestions pointing to a living and dynamic something, to "vibrating" forms. Heart-thinking lives in a wave-like semi-mathematical quality. The *Preface to the Revised 1918 Edition* and *Second Appendix* are written in the style and organic patterns of these models. A book or essay written in heart-thinking style imitates the lawfulnesses of organic growth, and the four levels of being. It is a thinking in perspectives and relationships.

---

[4] The German title is Die Philosophie der Freiheit which literally means the "Philosophy of Freehood." Steiner recommended the "Philosophy of Spiritual Activity" and there are several translations with this title (Lindeman and Stebbing). The most popular translation (Wilson) is called the Philosophy of Freedom. I prefer "freehood" over "freedom" or "spiritual activity" and I have an edited translation in the works called The Philosophy of Freehood.

[*] Dornach, the official representative body of Anthroposophy, has called 2006 the "year of the heart-thinking." Dornach's several publications on heart-thinking do not in fact describe what Steiner's method is.

In America, the situation is similar. The various Steiner presses and the Steiner Societies/Clubs avoid any concrete notions of heart-thinking. Even the Steiner translators group and the official Steiner Belle Letter Section in America and Dornach have no interest in his writing style except to offer the most astral praises.

The form of heart-thinking discussed here is the pioneering research effort of George O'Neil. O'Neil wrote some articles for the Anthroposophical Newsletter and countless notes and study guides one of which is available at the Steiner Library. George who certainly made a central discovery in Anthroposophy barely makes honorable mention in the recently published 700-page history of Anthroposophy in America by Barnes. Barnes worked with George for decades at the Branch in New York and could not recall any of George's work.

[5] My first encounter with heart-thinking came with Florin Lowndes' work in Germany. Lowndes was a student and friend of George O'Neil.

The first model is Goethe's archetypal plant.[6] All plants grow in seven stages (1. seed, 2. leaf, 3. bud, 4. flower, 5. pistil, 6. fruit, and 7. new seed). Each stage unfolds out of the other. The levels and steps of the plant reflect an inner organic lawfulness. In the diagram below we see that four laws of organic growth: 1. contraction and expansion (rhythm i.e., seed contracts, the leaf expands, the bud contracts etc.) 2. the increase in complexity of forms (enhancement or climb/swoop); 3. the mirroring (polarity); 4. the turning-inside-out (inversion).

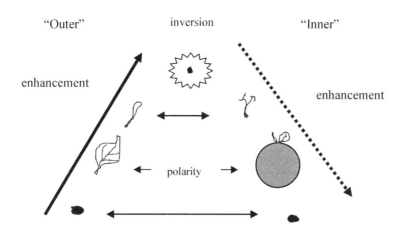

Similar in form to the archetypal plant, the seven-fold human being gives more substance, quality, and color to the four levels and their seven stages. The four basic levels of physical (form and content), life (method), astral (goal or design), and ego (essence or idea) and their corresponding questions (what, how, why, and who?) create the viewpoints of a heart-thinking thought-sequence. In the diagram below is the four-fold human being with its polar members (perspectives) of spirit-self (inner necessity), life-spirit (history or development), and spirit-man (new form and content).

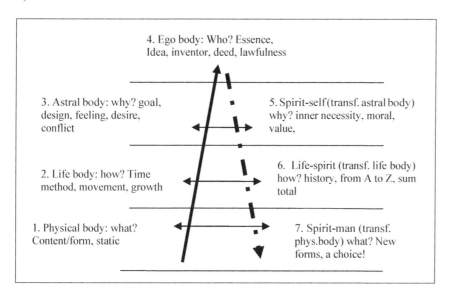

In this diagram one can see the lawful connections in the polarities contained on each of the levels. The laws of rhythm, enhancement, and inversion may take a little practice before they can be experienced as a reality. The reader must move from the whole to the parts, and from the parts to the whole, in order to grasp the flexible concepts of contraction and expansion, enhancement, and inversion. The organic laws are always unique to the situation. By comparing members of a sequence, by moving from the whole to the parts we begin to engage in organic heart-thinking.

---

[6] This form of the Urpflanze can be found in F. Lowndes Das Erwecken des Herz-denkens (Freies Geistesleben, 1999).

No text of Steiner's is so simple as to follow these models perfectly. One finds so many deviations, upside-down forms, winged forms, hard-to-crack forms. Nevertheless, our task is to see to what extent Steiner's work lives in the organic heart-thinking laws of enhancement and polarity.

II. How to Work with the Texts

Goal: The goal of this text work is to reach a place where one can move freely through the ideas of the text as if they were musical notes. Each text serves as a musical score. Every paragraph divides the thought-forms into sections. Each sentence elaborates the motif of the paragraph. The organic laws of rhythm, enhancement, polarity, and inversion become viewpoints from which we structure and restructure the idea-content of the text. We live in the in-between of the ideas. Our thinking has now gained four new laws and we begin to think with our hearts.

To See Thinking: Diagrams, lines and curves, colors and symbols help in the learning of heart-thinking. We sketch, make notes, draw diagrams, and distill the essentials. Ideas become close companions. We lift ourselves up high to abstractions in order live freely in ideas.

We seek to gain overviews of chapters and their sections. We read patterns and waves, interconnections. Every text becomes a living organism with a head, and a tail, with its own unique path.

Mortimer Adler wrote about reading a book for content and form. He suggests reading a book from the whole to the parts by comparing chapters, paragraphs, and sentences. By doing this we learn to see someone else's thinking. We need to imitate great ideas before we make them our own.

Preparation: But how do we get there?

Before working on a Steiner text a group needs to match and correct the English translation to a pre-1926 German edition of the original. The English translation will ideally include all grammatical aspects of the German original such as proper paragraph-, sentence-, and clause-count; and include Steiner's unique punctuation i.e., hyphen, asterix, and so on. Without a corrected text the exercise in heart-thinking shall remain arbitrary and confused.

The texts in this booklet have been translated, numbered, and the sentences have been indented. Several places may present difficulties for the reader:

In the *Preface to the Revised 1918 Edition*:
- the hyphen after paragraph 2/5 creates a new paragraph 3/1
- the parenthetical remark at the end of paragraph 5/5 is not part of the thought-form

In the *Second Appendix*:
- the Schiller quote in paragraph 2/4 belongs to sentence 2 in the sentence count thus there are four sentences in the paragraph
- the Fichte title in quotations in paragraph 6/6 has two sentences

Seeing the whole: Once the text has been checked the first step is to make synopses and condensements of each paragraph. We will start with *The Preface to the Revised 1918 Edition*. The goal is to have the content-outline of the whole preface on one sheet of paper. The synopses should grasp the skeleton of each paragraph, not all the details.[7]

The *Preface to the Revised 1918 Edition* has six paragraphs and the first paragraph has nine sentences. When reading one can circle key words, clarify difficult grammar, and note thematic breaks in the text. In the case of this paragraph the key words are "questions," "free will," and "soul." The thematic breaks come every three sentences.

1/9

1. There are two root-questions of the human soul-life toward which everything is directed that will be discussed in this book.

---

[7] See M. Adler's How to Read a Book, preferably the older edition. This book gives new understanding to the question of form and reading. It is a shame it is not required reading for Anthroposophists and Waldorf high school teachers.

2. The first question is whether there is a possibility to view the human being in such a way that this view proves itself to be the support for everything else which comes to meet the human being through experience or science and which gives him the feeling that it could not support itself.

3. Thereby one could easily be driven by doubt and critical judgment into the realm of uncertainty.

4. The other question is this: can the human being, as a creature of will, claim free will for himself, or is such freehood a mere illusion, which arises in him because he is not aware of the workings of necessity on which, as any other natural event, his will depends?

5. No artificial spinning of thoughts calls this question forth.

6. It comes to the soul quite naturally in a particular state of the soul.

7. And one can feel that something in the soul would decline, from what it should be, if it did not for once confront with the mightiest possible earnest questioning the two possibilities: freehood or necessity of will.

8. In this book it will be shown that the soul-experiences, which the human being must discover through the second question, depend upon which point of view he is able to take toward the first.

9. The attempt is made to prove that there is a certain view of the human being which can support his other knowledge; and furthermore, to point out that with this view a justification is won for the idea of freehood of will, if only that soul-region is first found in which free will can unfold itself.

Synopses of Paragraph 1/9:
Sentences 1-3: two questions, first question is about the view of human being
Sentences 4-6: the second question is about Freehood
Sentences 7-9: the second question depends on the first if soul-region is found

Final synopsis: "2 questions: the question of freehood depends on view of human being if soul-region is found"

The final synopsis sentence attempts to include the skeleton of the paragraph, not the individual details.
At this point we want to make simply an overview of the text, a kind of musical score where we know the general movement, but not necessarily the individual notes. Collecting all of the synopses on a sheet of paper we have in front of us a kind of master sheet from which all six paragraphs can be surveyed.

Catchwords		Preface 1918 Synopses
Two questions	1/9	Two questions: the freehood question depends on view of human being if soul region is found
Living answer	2/5	Not a theoretical answer memorized, but a living approach to reading the book
Value knowledge	3/1	A kind of knowledge which is correct and useful
Reader's value	4/10	Value for reader: foundation for science and spiritual knowledge if style of writing is grasped
Book changed	5/5	Steiner added sections and modernized vocabulary
2 books	6/6	No new philosophies in book, but a second book from the point of view of the first!

In the Synopsis of the Preface Diagram each paragraph is condensed into a sentence and further into a catchword. Notice how qualitatively each sentence fits nicely into the organic levels of the what, how, why, and who. (The who? is not represented directly by a paragraph.) We have completed the first step which is to have an overview of the text and compare the parts.

The Preface and the Four Laws: The task is to look now at the *Preface* from the point of view of the four laws: rhythm, enhancement, polarity, and inversion. The law of rhythm is, so to say accounted for by the questions: what? (contraction), how? (expansion), why? (contraction).[8]

The law of enhancement, or climb and swoop, can be found through applying the four questions. However, enhancement also implies that each paragraph becomes more inward, complicated, or intensified. Lowndes gives an example of intensification categories which are generally valid for Steiner's written works.[9] These are:

Categories of Enhancement:	Preface 1918:
1. Content and form	1. two questions
2. Method	2. read questions livingly
3. Design and desire	3. value for soul
4. Person and idea	
5. Moral aspect or necessity	4. foundation for spirituality
6. History or overview	5. history of book 1893 to 1918
7. New form	6. new book from original book

A question may arise whether or not these synopses have been stretched to fit the levels. The reader should then rework as many possible condensements and see what else arises. The question is only a good one once you have worked with the *Preface* for several weeks.

The third point of view is polarity. The structure of the four questions and their mirroring give the outline of polarity. Polarity is the contrast of the outer and inner aspects. In the *Preface* these are subtle gestures. The polarity between paragraphs 1/9 and 6/6 consists in the fact that 1/9 deals with the contents of the book (the outer aspect) and 6/6 deals with Steiner rethinking the contents (inner aspect). The polarity can be seen between in 2/5 method of reading the book and in 5/5 method of changing the book. The polar relationship between 3/1 (knowledge is correct and useful) and 4/10 (knowledge for science and spirituality) is found in their emphasis on the utility to the reader.

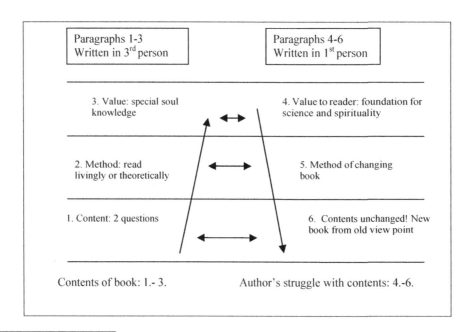

---

[8] But one can give further attention and even reverse the point of view: what? (expansion), how? (contraction) etc. These types of reversals are prevalent throughout this organic text. *There is often no one right point of view.*
[9] F. Lowndes, <u>The Enlivening of the Chakra of the Heart</u>

Inversion is the movement from outer to inner best represented by the Goethean Archetypal Plant. Michael Chekhov, a friend of Steiner's, pointed out that in every play there is a point in which the story takes a radical turn and winds down.[10] The first three paragraphs cover the contents of book; and paragraphs 4 through 6 explain the inner struggles that the author had with the two questions. Steiner captures this inversion through the introducing of the 1st person starting in paragraph 4/10. Through this grammatical subtlety the voice of the essay turns inward.

In Summation: The heart-thinking frame of mind tests Steiner's writing and thinking style by applying the organic laws to the text. At this stage we recognize that such a living thinking exists and that we develop a feel for the laws. In the next section a method of study will be described that when put into practice brings the thoughts into movement.

The Study Group: Traditionally, there are two steps to the study group: individual preparation and group presentation. The process requires that one first learns the content of the text by rewriting and rephrasing the sentences and then by viewing the enhancements and polarities. Presenting individual findings to the group allows people to hear and think through the unique phrasing of the other members. The directions given are an outline of various exercises which we lead to the goal of reproducing (forwards and backwards) the whole text sentence for sentence with a feel for the organic levels.

The first step is to read the text clearly and accurately. This means that everyone agrees on what is being said, but not necessarily in all its nuances. After the completion of a group reading and group synopsis of the *Preface's* paragraphs, we write the results on the board/paper as shown above. Whether for homework or at the study group, everyone is assigned a paragraph, or two, for rewriting in *their own words* to the extent this is possible by rephrasing the clauses! The goal at this point is *not to interpret* the *Preface* but to find synonyms and to explain what is written. The rewrites are presented to the group for comment and compliment.

The second step is to look for and prepare enhancements and polarities first at the paragraph and then at the sentence level. One method is to focus on and compare the word choice, grammar, and/or content in order to establish these lawfulnesses. (A list of various activities will be given at the end of this section encompassing varying levels of intensity.) When analyzing, for example, an enhancement from paragraph 1/9, to 2/5, to 3/1 one asks the question: what happens to the "two questions" in paragraphs 2/5 and 3/1? what point of view did Steiner present them from? The same sorts of questions are posed for the polarities: how are the "two questions" from paragraph 1/9 presented and how were they dealt with in 6/6? These simple questions can open up many perspectives and conclusions between group participants. The polarity and enhancement exercises eventually cover the individual sentences, more of which will be explained later in the chapter in detail.

The third step brings the participants into an organic state of consciousness. The participants present the entire text sentence for sentence within five minutes. The fast pace doesn't allow the presenter to think about the words, but instead allows them to live within the levels and streams of the text. The wave-forms are, at this level, second nature, the participants naturally see the levels, polarities, and they hear the "turning points" because certain words and intonations in context move the reader to feel organic form.[11]

The Nine Thought-Forms of the Preface and Second Appendix: There are nine main thought-forms. Steiner included them in these two Prefaces. This is proof of their unique status in the corpus of his work. He gave the keys to the book. Every other form is a combination of them.

People have asked whether there are other forms. Beyond the nine, Lowndes lists about 30 other forms. The booklet covers the basic nine which are a prerequisite to working with Steiner's other books.

In the text examples of this section I included as many catch-words as necessary in order to make the levels and polarities readily comprehensible. The text precedes the diagram for quick reference. Keep in mind there is no perfect synopsis.

Here are the basic nine forms with the addition of 12- and 13-form. Note in the 13-form how the zigzag is connected at the bottom. In this way, one could construct a 17-, 21-, 25-, or 29-form. Connected 7-forms make up

---

[10] M. Chekov, To the Actor

[11] Very few people have had the power to reach this level, and often their lack of faith prevents this experience. Students and friends of mine without any prior contact to Steiner's works seem to have the necessary vigor. I sometimes wonder if a person who has too much contact with Steiner's work doesn't loose his vitality.

a 13-form as well as 19-, 25-, and 31-forms respectively. Unique in all the forms is the 12-form as it does not follow the law of symmetry. Mirroring forms (6- and 8-forms) cannot be connected!

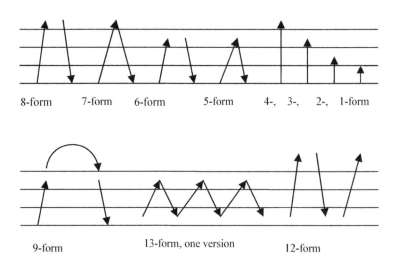

These are some alternative form. Rare, but extant, are the upside-down forms which begin at the ego level and descend to the physical level. Then there are the winged forms, the most common being the 11-form which is a classical 9-form with wings i.e., an extra blue level paragraph/sentence before and after the main form.

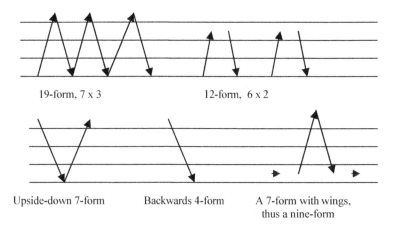

The Main forms of the Preface and Second Appendix: The *Preface* form of 6 paragraphs has been displayed several times so far. In the *Second Appendix* displayed below we see two interlocking seven-forms with a total of thirteen paragraphs. When placed next to one another, similar themes can be glimpsed as Steiner basically says the same thing but from different perspectives.

Both texts cover the topics of thinking, knowing, science, freehood, and method of the book.[12] We can explore similarities of themes. It is really amazing to take note of the subtle repetitions for it is exactly these that make the text(s) organic-living.

---

[12] In seminars Florin Lowndes has done some exercises with the two Prefaces in which he superimposes one on top of the other.

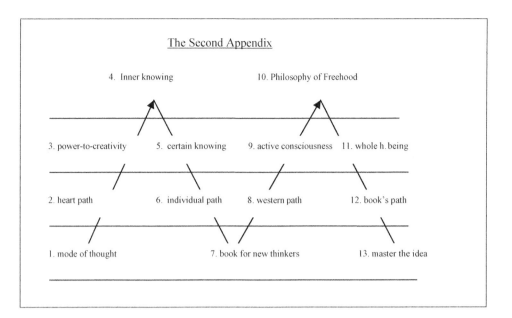

The Second Appendix

4. Inner knowing   10. Philosophy of Freehood

3. power-to-creativity   5. certain knowing   9. active consciousness   11. whole h. being

2. heart path   6. individual path   8. western path   12. book's path

1. mode of thought   7. book for new thinkers   13. master the idea

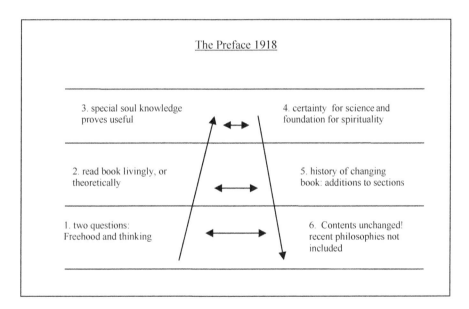

The Preface 1918

3. special soul knowledge   4. certainty for science and
proves useful   foundation for spirituality

2. read book livingly, or   5. history of changing
theoretically   book: additions to sections

1. two questions: 6. Contents unchanged!
Freehood and thinking   recent philosophies not
                                 included

Text Examples: This 4-form is from paragraph 11/4 of the *Second Appendix*. The main topic in each of these sentences revolves around the value of science. Each sentence answers the questions of the levels quite clearly.

11/4

1. All scientific endeavors would be only a satisfying of idle curiosity, if they did not strive toward uplifting the *existential worth of the human personality.*
2. The sciences attain their true value only by demonstrating the human significance of their results.
3. Not the refinement of any single capacity of soul can be the final goal of individuality, but rather the development of all the faculties slumbering within us.
4. Knowledge only has value when it contributes to the all sided unfolding of the *whole* human nature.

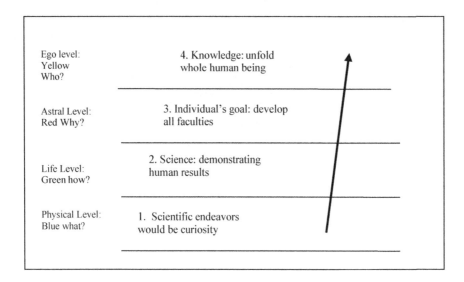

Ego level:
Yellow
Who?

4. Knowledge: unfold
   whole human being

Astral Level:
Red Why?

3. Individual's goal: develop
   all faculties

Life Level:
Green how?

2. Science: demonstrating
   human results

Physical Level:
Blue what?

1. Scientific endeavors
   would be curiosity

This next example is from paragraph is 1/3 of the *Second Appendix*. (The fourth or ego level is not represented directly by a sentence.) Each sentence clearly embodies the levels, particularly the astral or 3rd sentence filled with feeling and conflict. Grammatically, this paragraph has a classical pattern of passive verb (will be reproduced), active verb (placed), and model auxiliary (want).

1/3
1. In what follows will be reproduced in all its essentials that which stood as a kind of "preface" in the first edition of this book.
2. I placed it here as an "appendix," since it reflects the type of thinking in which I wrote it twenty-five years ago, and not because it adds to the content of the book.
3. I did not want to leave it out completely for the simple reason, that time and again the opinion surfaces that I have something to suppress of my earlier writings because of my later spiritual writings.

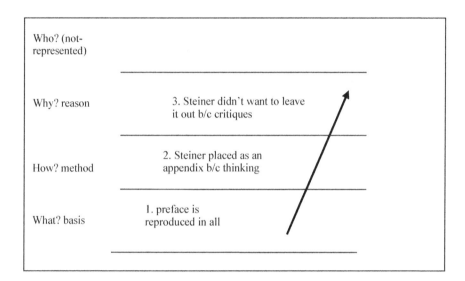

Paragraph 1/9 of the *Preface to the revised 1918 Edition* is a very special form in Steiner's work. The nine-fold human being requires a little study. The ego level of the seven-fold human being is subdivided into the three souls. Thus, sentences four, five and six are on the ego level.

(The topic shifts every 3 sentences. The ego level sentences share the same topic (the freehood question). Sentence four answers the question why?, sentence five how?, and sentence six what? There is also a kind of polarity between sentence one and six, two and five, three and four.)

In addition to the three-foldness of the structure is the polar nature of the nine-form. The first four sentences present the "questions" while sentences five through nine address the conditions under which the questions can be addressed. Therefore one can enter into promise of the book if one fulfills these requirements:

- If one has reached a particular soul state
- If one has confronted their own Freehood
- If one is capable of the right point of view of the human being
- If one finds the soul region for unfolding free will

Most people are not interested in freehood and the reason is according to Steiner that they have not reached that level of maturity or "Freiheitsmoment" in this lifetime. The problem then is to find the right viewing or thinking. What is this soul region? It is not the soul region of logical thinking or the rational soul. Steiner gives little hints throughout the *Preface to the Revised 1918 Edition* on how to find this soul region.

1/9

1. There are two root-questions of the human soul-life toward which everything is directed that will be discussed in this book.

2. The first question is whether there is a possibility to view the human being in such a way that this view proves itself to be the support for everything else which comes to meet the human being through experience or science and which gives him the feeling that it could not support itself.

3. Thereby one could easily be driven by doubt and critical judgment into the realm of uncertainty.

4. The other question is this: can the human being, as a creature of will, claim free will for himself, or is such freehood a mere illusion, which arises in him because he is not aware of the workings of necessity on which, as any other natural event, his will depends?

5. No artificial spinning of thoughts calls this question forth.

6. It comes to the soul quite naturally in a particular state of the soul.

7. And one can feel that something in the soul would decline, from what it should be, if it did not for once confront with the mightiest possible earnest questioning the two possibilities: freehood or necessity of will.

8. In this book it will be shown that the soul-experiences, which the human being must discover through the second question, depend upon which point of view he is able to take toward the first.

9. The attempt is made to prove that there is a certain view of the human being which can support his other knowledge; and furthermore, to point out that with this view a justification is won for the idea of freehood of will, if only that soul-region is first found in which free will can unfold itself.

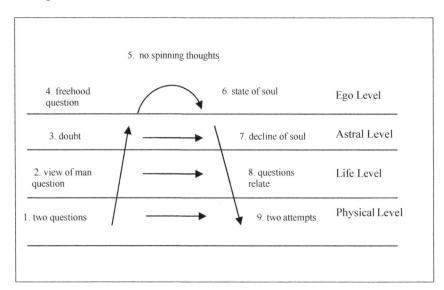

Next to paragraph 1/9 *Preface*, paragraph 9/16 of the *Second Appendix* contains some of the most essential information about the nature of the heart-thinking. Steiner argues that the way to wholeness is to take the elements of science and relate them in a artistic-musical-compositional manner and thereby develop a new idea consciousness, a compositional-consciousness! Thus the goal of the book is make consciousness itself organic living. So simple and fun.

The polarities in 9/16 are based on a 'problem and solution' model. For example in sentence 1 the 'problem' is the "many realms of life", in sentence 8 the solution is the composer (he who brings the elements into a whole). Between sentence 2 and 7 the polarity is: the "sciences" find their compliment in the arts; between sentences 3 and 6, the old specialized sciences find their fulfillment in a "new science" arising out of their results. The problem of wholeness in knowing in sentence 4 finds its solution in the organic science of sentence 5.

These polarities are subtle and they can be continued even to include the second half of 9/16.

9/16

1. There are many realms of life.
2. Every single one has developed a particular science for itself.
3. Life itself, however, is a unity and the more the sciences are striving to research in their own specialized areas the more they distance themselves from the view of the living unity of the world.
4. There must be a type of knowing that seeks in the specialized 'sciences' that which is necessary to lead us back once more to the wholeness of life.
5. The specialized researcher wants through his own knowledge to gain an understanding of the world and its workings; in this book the goal is a philosophical one: science shall itself become organic-living.
6. The specialized sciences are preliminary stages of the science striven for here.
7. A similar relationship predominates in the arts.
8. The composer works on the basis of the theory of composition.
9. The latter is the sum of knowledge whose possession is a necessary precondition of composing.
10. In composing, the laws of the theory of composition serve life itself, serve actual reality.
11. In exactly the same sense, philosophy is a creative *art*.
12. All genuine philosophers are *concept-artists*.
13. Through them, human ideas became artistic materials and the scientific method became artistic technique.
14. Thereby, abstract thinking gains concrete, individual life.
15. Ideas become life-powers.
16. We have then not just a knowing about things but we have made knowing instead into an actual, self- governing organism; our authentic, active consciousness has placed itself above a mere passive receiving of truths.

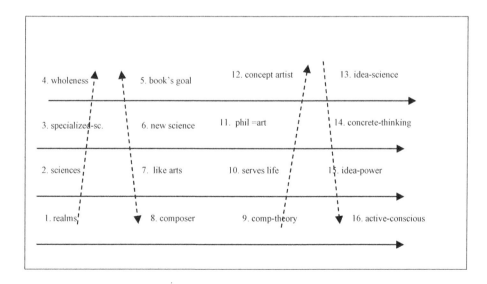

Below is the first seven paragraphs of the *Second Appendix*. The content deals with the inner path to truth and what this truth is. The *Second Appendix* itself consists of two connected 7-forms. The first 7-form follows the organic schema clearly: what? The preface; how? the heart-path; why? to gain our individual power; who? We want inner knowing.

Even the polarities are clear: what? 1/3 the preface and 7/5 the book; how? 2/4 Schiller's path and 6/6 Fichte's path; why? 3/3 Truth and 5/3 knowledge from experience; 4/4 is the turning point who? Inner knowing.

The use of the pronoun "we" from paragraphs 4/4 to 7/5 is also of the indicators of the inversion process. There are many such devices Steiner used throughout his work.

The Second Appendix [to the Philosophy of Freehood]

1/3

1. In what follows will be reproduced in all its essentials that which stood as a kind of "preface" in the first edition of this book. 2. I placed it here as an "appendix," since it reflects the type of thinking in which I wrote it twenty-five years ago, and not because it adds to the content of the book. 3. I did not want to leave it out completely for the simple reason, that time and again the opinion surfaces that I have something to suppress of my earlier writings because of my later spiritual writings.

2/4

1. Our age can only want to draw *truth* out of the depths of man's being. 2. Of Schiller's well-known two paths:

"Truth seek we both, you in outer life, I within

In the heart, and each will find it for sure.

Is the eye healthy so it meets the Creator outside;

Is the heart healthy then it reflects inwardly the World"

the present age will benefit more from the second. 3. A truth that comes to us from the outside always carries the stamp of uncertainty. 4. Only what appears as truth to each and every one of us in his own inner being is what we want to believe.

3/3

1. Only truth can bring us certainty in the development of our individual powers. 2. Whoever is tormented by doubt his powers are lamed. 3. In a world that is puzzling to him he can find no goal for his creativity.

4/4

1. We no longer want merely to *believe*; we want to *know*. 2. Belief requires the accepting of truths, which we cannot fully grasp. 3. However, what we do not fully grasp undermines our individuality, which wants to experience everything with its deepest inner being. 4. Only that *knowing* satisfies us that subjects itself to no external norms, but springs instead out of the inner life of the personality.

5/3

1. We also do not want a form of knowing, which is fixed for all eternity in rigid academic rules and is kept in compendia valid for all time. 2. We hold that each of us is justified in starting from firsthand experiences, from immediate life conditions, and from there climbing to a knowledge of the whole universe. 3. We strive for certainty in knowing, but each in his own unique way.

6/6

1. Our scientific theories should also no longer take the position that our acceptance of them was a matter of absolute coercion. 2. None of us would give a title to an academic work such as *Fichte* once did: "A Crystal Clear Report to the Public at Large on the Actual Nature of Modern Philosophy. 3. *An Attempt to Compel Readers to Understand.*" 4. Today nobody should be compelled to understand. 5. We are not asking for acceptance or agreement from anyone who is not driven by a specific need to form his own personal worldview. 6. Nowadays we also do not want to cram knowledge into the unripe human being, the child, instead we try to develop his faculties so that he will not have to be *compelled* to understand, but *will* want to understand.

7/5

1. I am under no illusion in regard to this characteristic of my time. 2. I know that generic mass-ified culture [individualitaetloses Schablonentum] lives and spreads itself throughout society. 3. But I know just as well that many of my contemporaries seek to set up their lives according to the direction indicated here. 4. To them I want to dedicate this work. 5. It should not lead down "the only possible" path to truth, but it should *tell* about the path one has taken, for whom truth is what it is all about.

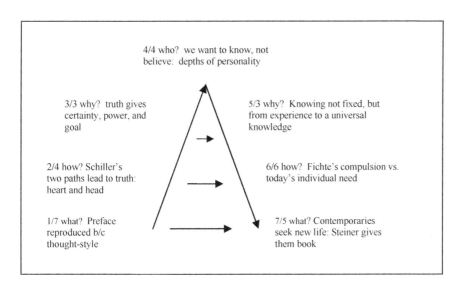

4/4 who? we want to know, not believe: depths of personality

3/3 why? truth gives certainty, power, and goal

5/3 why? Knowing not fixed, but from experience to a universal knowledge

2/4 how? Schiller's two paths lead to truth: heart and head

6/6 how? Fichte's compulsion vs. today's individual need

1/7 what? Preface reproduced b/c thought-style

7/5 what? Contemporaries seek new life: Steiner gives them book

84

Paragraph 2/5 of the *Preface to the revised 1918 Edition* discusses how the question of the view of the human being can be answered by its integration, not memorization. The first two sentences present the "view" in its un-integrated form. In contrast the last two sentences present the "view" in its living, integrated form. Sentence 3 states that the type of thinking, organic-living, is the foundation of the book.

Sentence 1 and 5 create a solid polarity: the not-yet-integrated view of sentence one is integrated into the soul in sentence five. The theoretical memorized answer of sentence 2 becomes a living soul activity in sentence four. This paragraph is an excellent model for writing exercises because of the clarity of the polarities.

2/5

1. The view, which is under discussion here in reference to these two questions, presents itself as one that, once attained, can be integrated as a member of the truly living soul life.
2. There is no theoretical answer given that, once acquired, can be carried about as a conviction merely preserved in the memory.
3. This kind of answer would be only an illusory one for the type of thinking which is the foundation of this book.
4. Not such a finished, fixed answer is given, rather a definite region of soul-experience is referred to, in which one may, through the inner activity of the soul itself, answer the question livingly anew at any moment he requires.
5. The true view of this region will give the one who eventually finds the soul-sphere where these questions unfold that which he needs for these two riddles of life, so that he may, so empowered, enter further into the widths and depths of this enigmatic human life, into which need and destiny impel him to wander.

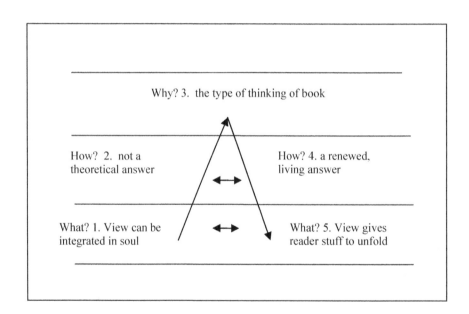

Some Additional Thoughts on Text Study: There are several tempos and intensity of group work. When the group decides that it will not do outside preparation and in-group presentations, then it meets for the purpose of making synopses of the paragraphs and discussing some of the polarities. Once a group commits to 8 meetings with preparation and presentations then the 3-step model above is appropriate. The group needs to distribute the work over the eight meetings and make a syllabus so that everyone is on the same page. I found that repeating assignments often held the group together because only work and experience can bring clarity to the meditation. Here is a typical study group syllabus[13] designed for one group leader and 5 participants:

8 meetings (1 hour 20 minutes for each meeting):

These meetings are best led by someone who has done the work already. Sometimes group study can be messy and having someone responsible can bring the group forward especially with those who are prone to distraction or arguing. Thus a kind of group leader should help the others into the exercise. "Group leader" means in this sense a keeper of good manners rather then a know-it-all.

1. The group reads aloud the Preface 1918. Then after reading a paragraph the group members summarized and offer synopses. The members agree on which synopses are best. The group leader writes these condensements on the board.

   Homework: Each participant rewrites two paragraphs clause for clause. Try to include key words and keep the same number of clauses. The goal is to present the paragraphs in such a way that the other participants listen to content being repeated in slightly different wording however with the same clause-rhythm. Thus in preparation for the second meeting everyone should be ready to read aloud their rewrite/rephrasing of the paragraphs.

2. Start the second meeting by listening to the assigned presentations. The members give feedback on the completeness of the presentations or discuss difficult passages. Next the leader gives pointers on how to prepare the enhancements and polarities presentations.

   Homework: Polarity and enhancement assignments are given to the five participants. Participants prepare for example the enhancement of paragraphs 1/9, 2/5, and 3/1 of the Preface 1918 or a polarity between 1/9 and 6/6.

3. The group may choose a blackboard for their presentations since the forms are easier to see. The leader discusses organic laws at the sentence level.

   Homework: The group picks two paragraphs for the presentation of polarities at the sentence level.

4. The group presents polarities on the board. Now the group rereads the Preface 1918 but, this time, underlines the main clauses in each sentence. A grammar book might help.

   Homework: finish underlining main clauses.

5. Discuss and finish the clause work. Start making catchwords for each sentence. The catchword can be a word from the sentence itself, but doesn't have to be.

   Homework: Find a catch-phrase for every sentence in the *Preface*. Put them in organic diagram form.

6. Discuss and share the catchwords/phrases for each sentence. Agree on a group catchword for all of the sentences.

   Homework: Participants should prepare two paragraphs and present the contents of each sentence from the catch-words only!

7. Listen to presentations. Discuss to what extent the form and color helps you to see the content?!

   Homework: Prepare to present the whole Preface 1918 from the catch-words with a 5 minute time limit.

8. Listen and enjoy presentations. Try presenting the Preface 1918 as if the last sentence was first. Congratulate yourselves!

Intensive Study: After the group has mastered the form and content of the *Preface* and repeated the thought-forms 50 times (preferably alone at home), it may opt for even more intensive work. This next process requires an in-depth analysis of the word choice in each individual sentence. One basically makes four columns and places each word of a sentence into one of the columns: nouns, verbs, adjectives, and adverbs. Thus one can survey all of the words and make note of certain patterns such as: the first sentences usually have a predominance of passive verbs, second sentences active verbs, third sentences conditional verbs and so on. Each text has its own unique word choice or grammar structure. This exercise is excellent for learning to write organically.

From this exercise, the group can start working on writing their synopses in organic style. For example, blue paragraphs might have more passive verbs, green paragraphs more active verbs, red paragraphs might be

---

[13] These instructions are loosely based on various exercises F. Lowndes gave to our study group years ago. I tweaked them over the years to fit the needs of individual groups.

written with more feeling or intellect. These exercises bring the heart-thinking out of its meditative form and place it into the realm of an actual technique.

The style of writing is also a style of speaking. Speaking the text according to the colors can be quite an experience. At first it seems a little artificial but there is much room for artistic creativity. The speech should make the organic laws audible.

Heart-thinking as it relates to Imagination, Inspiration, and Intuition: F. Lowndes outlines four meditative aspects of the heart-thinking work in his <u>Das Erwecken des Herz-Denkens</u>. The first aspect he calls *precise perception of the text and its organization*. That is why the text must be an exact translation and why the synopses and diagrams are so essential. The text becomes our own garden in which we can see all the rows, colors, and gestalt.

The second aspect is the walking through the garden. We walk and *view the fixed thought forms that constitute the path of the text*. Some chapters have as many as 52 paragraphs and involve "something like a dream experience… the subjective experience can become lived as something stretched out over a longer time while the clock time in reality shows that only seconds have passed." Lowndes continues that meditating on the whole book, <u>Philosophy of Spiritual Activity</u>, backwards and forwards, we come to the point of experiencing our own role in shaping the thought forms by ourselves. We become, thereby, one with the text and speak with the author!

The third aspect of text work is to move yourself into the growing and unfolding thoughts while *listening to the unfolding melody and rhythm until one lives into the thought-breathing and - pulsing*. Lowndes says that we connect the living thought process with the heart and the rhythmic system of physical life and make conscious the thought activity of the etheric life. "Our way through the garden expresses itself and concentrates on the *going* itself, on the separate qualities of each curve…these qualities cannot be experienced at the same time…." The succession is experienced not in space, but in time. This experience of the organic form Lowndes emphasizes is a feeling experience more imaginative than picture-like, and therefore a more inspired level of meditation. It is at this point that one starts practical work such as composing one's own organic-living speaking and writing forms.

The fourth aspect of text work is the individual level in which the meditator and the being of Intuition are mixed together. The fourth level *is a state of grace in which we meditate pure being*, that is, pure substance without form, pure thought-rhythm without thought, pure activity without thought form, or simply put, pure becoming. "In the imaginative level we see the thought form, the what, just as a finished picture; in the inspirational level we live in the living process, the how, just as we follow the origination of a picture from a living process; in the intuitive level we finally live in the will impulses, even before it has taken any form, and we know the "why" of the thought organism just as it is lived, the "why" of the thought form just as it is taking form."

Two Texts of the Philosophy of Freehood:

PREFACE TO THE REVISED 1918 EDITION

1/9

1. There are two root-questions of the human soul-life toward which everything is directed that will be discussed in this book.

2. The first question is whether there is a possibility to view the human being in such a way that this view proves itself to be the support for everything else which comes to meet the human being through experience or science and which gives him the feeling that it could not support itself.

3. Thereby one could easily be driven by doubt and critical judgment into the realm of uncertainty.

4. The other question is this: can the human being, as a creature of will, claim free will for himself, or is such freehood a mere illusion, which arises in him because he is not aware of the workings of necessity on which, as any other natural event, his will depends?

5. No artificial spinning of thoughts calls this question forth.

6. It comes to the soul quite naturally in a particular state of the soul.

7. And one can feel that something in the soul would decline, from what it should be, if it did not for once confront with the mightiest possible earnest questioning the two possibilities: freehood or necessity of will.

8. In this book it will be shown that the soul-experiences, which the human being must discover through the second question, depend upon which point of view he is able to take toward the first.

9. The attempt is made to prove that there is a certain view of the human being which can support his other knowledge; and furthermore, to point out that with this view a justification is won for the idea of freehood of will, if only that soul-region is first found in which free will can unfold itself.

2/5

1. The view, which is under discussion here in reference to these two questions, presents itself as one that, once attained, can be integrated as a member of the truly living soul life.

2. There is no theoretical answer given that, once acquired, can be carried about as a conviction merely preserved in the memory.

3. This kind of answer would be only an illusory one for the type of thinking which is the foundation of this book.

4. Not such a finished, fixed answer is given, rather a definite region of soul-experience is referred to, in which one may, through the inner activity of the soul itself, answer the question livingly anew at any moment he requires.

5. The true view of this region will give the one who eventually finds the soul-sphere where these questions unfold that which he needs for these two riddles of life, so that he may, so empowered, enter further into the widths and depths of this enigmatic human life, into which need and destiny impel him to wander.

3/1

1. - A kind of knowledge seems thereby to be pointed to which, through its own inner life and by the connectedness of this inner life to the whole life of the human soul, proves its correctness and usefulness.

4/10

1. This is what I thought about the content of the book when I wrote it down twenty-five years ago.

2. Today, too, I have to write down such sentences if I want to characterize the purpose of the thoughts of this book.

3. At the original writing I limited myself to say no more than that, which in the *utmost closest sense* is connected with the two basic questions, referred to here.

4. If someone should be amazed that he finds in the book no reference to that region of the world of spiritual experience which came to expression in my later writings, he should bear in mind that in those days I did not however want to give a description of results of spiritual research but I wanted to build first the foundation on which such results could rest.

5. This Philosophy of Freehood does not contain any such specific spiritual results any *more* than it contains specific results of other fields of knowledge; but he who strives to attain certainty for such cognition cannot, in my view, ignore that which it does indeed contain.

6. What is said in the book can be acceptable to anyone who, for whatever reasons of his own, does not want anything to do with the results of my spiritual scientific research.

7. To the one, however, who can regard these spiritual scientific results, as something toward which he is attracted, what has been attempted here will also be important.

8. It is this: to prove how an open-minded consideration of these two questions which are fundamental for *all* knowing, leads to the view that the human being *lives* in a true spiritual world.

9. In this book the attempt is made to justify cognition of the spiritual world *before* entering into actual spiritual experience.

10. And this justification is so undertaken that in these chapters one need not look at my later valid experiences in order to find acceptable what is said here, if one is able or wants to enter into the particular style of the writing itself.

5/5

1. Thus it seems to me that this book on the one hand assumes a position completely independent of my actual spiritual scientific writings; yet on the other hand it also stands in the closest possible connection to them.

2. These considerations brought me now, after twenty-five years, to republish the content of the text almost completely unchanged in all essentials.

3. I have only made somewhat longer additions to a number of sections.

4. The experiences I made with the incorrect interpretations of what I said caused me to publish comprehensive commentaries.

5. I changed only those places where what I said a quarter of a century ago seemed to me inappropriately formulated for the present time.

(Only a person wanting to discredit me could find occasion on the basis of the changes made *in this way*, to say that I have changed my fundamental conviction.)

6/6

1. The book has been sold out for many years.

2. I nevertheless hesitated for a long time with the completion of this new edition and it seems to me, in following the line of thought in the previous section, that today the same should be expressed which I asserted twenty-five years ago in reference to these questions.

3. I have asked myself again and again whether I might, or not, discuss several topics of the numerous contemporary philosophical views put forward since the publication of the first edition.

4. To do this in a way acceptable to me was impossible in recent times because of the demands of my pure spiritual scientific research.

5. Yet I have convinced myself now after a most intense review of present day philosophical work, that as tempting as such a discussion in itself would be, it is for what should be said through my book, not to be included in the same.

6. What seemed to me necessary to say, from the point of view of the Philosophy of Freehood about the most recent philosophical directions can be found in the second volume of my Riddles of Philosophy.

April 1918   Rudolf Steiner

THE SECOND APPENDIX [to the <u>Philosophy of Freehood</u>]

1/3
1. In what follows will be reproduced in all its essentials that which stood as a kind of "preface" in the first edition of this book.
2. I placed it here as an "appendix," since it reflects the type of thinking in which I wrote it twenty-five years ago, and not because it adds to the content of the book.
3. I did not want to leave it out completely for the simple reason, that time and again the opinion surfaces that I have something to suppress of my earlier writings because of my later spiritual writings.

2/4
1. Our age can only want to draw *truth* out of the depths of man's being.[**]
2. Of Schiller's well-known two paths:
> "Truth seek we both, you in outer life, I within
> In the heart, and each will find it for sure.
> Is the eye healthy so it meets the Creator outside;
> Is the heart healthy then it reflects inwardly the World"
the present age will benefit more from the second.
3. A truth that comes to us from the outside always carries the stamp of uncertainty.
4. Only what appears as truth to each and every one of us in his own inner being is what we want to believe.

3/3
1. Only truth can bring us certainty in the development of our individual powers.
2. Whoever is tormented by doubt his powers are lamed.
3. In a world that is puzzling to him he can find no goal for his creativity.

4/4
1. We no longer want merely to *believe*; we want to *know*.
2. Belief requires the accepting of truths, which we cannot fully grasp.
3. However, what we do not fully grasp undermines our individuality, which wants to experience everything with its deepest inner being.
4. Only that *knowing* satisfies us that subjects itself to no external norms, but springs instead out of the inner life of the personality.

5/3
1. We also do not want a form of knowing, which is fixed for all eternity in rigid academic rules and is kept in compendia valid for all time.
2. We hold that each of us is justified in starting from firsthand experiences, from immediate life conditions, and from there climbing to a knowledge of the whole universe.
3. We strive for certainty in knowing, but each in his own unique way.

6/6
1. Our scientific theories should also no longer take the position that our acceptance of them was a matter of absolute coercion.
2. None of us would give a title to an academic work such as *Fichte* once did: "A Crystal Clear Report to the Public at Large on the Actual Nature of Modern Philosophy.
3. *An Attempt to Compel Readers to Understand.*"
4. Today nobody should be compelled to understand.
5. We are not asking for acceptance or agreement from anyone who is not driven by a specific need to form his own personal worldview.

[**] Only the first introductory paragraphs have been completely omitted from this work, which today appear to me totally unessential. What is said in the remaining paragraphs however, seems to me necessary to say in the present because of and in spite of the natural scientific manner of thinking of our contemporaries.

6. Nowadays we also do not want to cram knowledge into the unripe human being, the child, instead we try to develop his faculties so that he will not have to be *compelled* to understand, but *will* want to understand.

7/5

1. I am under no illusion in regard to this characteristic of my time.
2. I know that generic mass-ified culture [individualitaetloses Schablonentum] lives and spreads itself throughout society.
3. But I know just as well that many of my contemporaries seek to set up their lives according to the direction indicated here.
4. To them I want to dedicate this work.
5. It should not lead down "the only possible" path to truth, but it should *tell* about the path one has taken, for whom truth is what it is all about.

8/6

1. The book leads at first into more abstract spheres where thought must take on sharp contours in order to come to certain points.
2. However, the reader will be led out of these dry concepts and into concrete life.
3. I am certainly of the opinion that one must lift oneself into the ether world of concepts, if one wants to penetrate existence in all directions.
4. He who only knows how to have pleasure through his senses, doesn't know life's finest pleasures.
5. The eastern masters have their disciples spend years in a life of renunciation and asceticism before they disclose to them what they themselves know.
6. The West no longer requires pious practices and ascetic exercises for scientific knowledge, but what is needed instead is the good will that leads to withdrawing oneself for short periods of time from the firsthand impressions of life and entering into the spheres of the pure thought world.

9/16

1. There are many realms of life.
2. Every single one has developed a particular science for itself.
3. Life itself, however, is a unity and the more the sciences[*] are striving to research in their own specialized areas the more they distance themselves from the view of the living unity of the world.
4. There must be a type of knowing that seeks in the specialized 'sciences' that which is necessary to lead us back once more to the wholeness of life.
5. The specialized researcher wants through his own knowledge to gain an understanding of the world and its workings; in this book the goal is a philosophical one: science shall itself become organic-living.
6. The specialized sciences are preliminary stages of the science striven for here.
7. A similar relationship predominates in the arts.
8. The composer works on the basis of the theory of composition.
9. The latter is the sum of knowledge whose possession is a necessary precondition of composing.
10. In composing, the laws of the theory of composition serve life itself, serve actual reality.
11. In exactly the same sense, philosophy is a creative *art*.
12. All genuine philosophers are *concept-artists*.
13. Through them, human ideas became artistic materials and the scientific method became artistic technique.
14. Thereby, abstract thinking gains concrete, individual life.
15. Ideas become life-powers.
16. We have then not just a knowing about things but we have made knowing instead into an actual, self-governing organism; our authentic, active consciousness has placed itself above a mere passive receiving of truths.

---

[*] [Translator's note: The term "Wissenschaften" means in German the "sciences" and the term includes for example the science of biology, the science of chemistry as well as the science of history, the science of music, and the science psychology. Thus the English term needs to be more inclusive. Steiner used such words as "science", "knowledge", and "knowing" in very unique ways with varying meanings dependent of course on the context.]

10/3

1. How philosophy as art relates to the *freehood* of the human being, what freehood is, and whether we are active in our freehood or able to become active: this is the main question of my book.

2. All other scientific explanations are included here only because they provide an explanation, in my opinion, about those things that are of importance to human beings.

3. A "*Philosophy of Freehood*" shall be given in these pages.

11/4

1. All scientific endeavors would be only a satisfying of idle curiosity, if they did not strive toward uplifting the *existential worth of the human personality.*

2. The sciences attain their true value only by demonstrating the human significance of their results.

3. Not the refinement of any single capacity of soul can be the final goal of individuality, but rather the development of all the faculties slumbering within us.

4. Knowledge only has value when it contributes to the *all sided* unfolding of the *whole* human nature.

12/1

1. This book, therefore, conceives the relationship between scientific knowledge and life not in such a way that man has to bow down before the idea and consecrate his forces to its service, but rather in the sense that man masters the world of ideas in order to make use of it for his *human* goals, which transcend the mere scientific.

13/1

1. One must experience and place oneself consciously above the idea; *otherwise* one falls into its servitude.

Miscellaneous Notes

Understanding Waldorf education: The Primer outlines a new vision of human development and pedagogy, aspects of which have been realized in Waldorf education. According to Steiner our ability to grow wise and productive with age depends on our preschool education, and on an individual's commitment to self-education. Steiner's vision of childhood education attempts to address the growing person without imposing any ideology. He believed in providing only what strengthens our youth forces so that by age twenty-one, we have a foundation which aids us in carrying on our own personal path.

Who needs the vision the Primer offers? Really all children do! There is an obvious and unhealthy trend in education to curtail childhood by intensifying repetitive drill, "medicating", de-personalizing, and standardizing school. No one is immune to this type of practice, even more heart-felt educators (heart-math, dyslexia specialists, and some modern Waldorf schools) teach the mechanical drill method, and continue to work out of the old assumptions that all children must have the basics by age seven. Much of the theory and practice of alternative, holistic, reform, and Indigo education still lives in the spirit of corporate models of education.[14] The purpose of the Primer is to create a healthy educational environment, and to give the teachers a new soul gesture, which encourages children to unfold at their own pace.

The Primer is systematic. Steiner presents many coalescing viewpoints on human development and spirituality in this essay. Each paragraph could be expanded into a larger essay. The Primer states that children bring the fruit and pain of past-lives. Children need dance, a spirit of reverence, carefully spoken words, and energy work in order to thrive. Loving and joyful behavior on the part of the teacher help the children to keep in balance their willing, feeling, thinking, and intuition. Each seven-year cycle has a distinct and unique educational task and the earlier years are crucial to the development of freedom in the individual's life time. The Primer has a special organic-form that helps teachers live into a new dynamic heart-thinking essential to a new type of lessons.

The Primer gives the foundation for Steiner's later educational lectures and aids greatly in their comprehension. The Primer presents an education according to seven-year cycles, while the Waldorf lectures are based on 2 1/3 year cycles i.e., teaching method changes every two years. The information in the Primer is expanded upon in his lectures. For example, Steiner suggests two foreign languages, knitting, painting, movement, farming, and music classes, not simply as "add-ons," but as an integral part of Waldorf education. Steiner created the "block system" in which students spend two hours a day on one subject for four weeks: the first month they have a block of chemistry, the next month math, and then geography and so on. It is of utmost importance that one teacher teaches all of these blocks in the elementary school because a teacher that is connected to his students can guide them wholly in their paths. These are the basics of Waldorf, not its ideal.

The ideas of the Primer combined with Steiner's concrete suggestions realized in the Waldorf School, give enough indications to found an altogether new school. Many authors have distilled the principles of Waldorf education so that a new school could be founded on those principles.[15] The inner work in heart-thinking, the organic coordination of the main lessons and skills classes, the teaching of heart-thinking by way of example, healing work for teachers that addresses all four bodies; these would be the new pillars of a renewed Waldorf education.[16]

---

[14] Corporate and some forms of State directed education have several insidious ways of working. The first is to disable the intellect by excluding philosophy or books that sharpen the mind. The second way is to weaken the will or volition of the pupils. This can be done in spite of having a challenging curriculum as is the case in academically challenging public and boarding schools. The will of the child can be easily pacified, or rechanneled, e.g., by promising a wealthy and stable future, if only the students will comply until the end of graduate school. The damage is already done by the first three grades of elementary school according to Gatto.

[15] A list of literature, and even summaries of Steiner's educational lectures, can be found at www.waldorfbooks.org particularly in the section called "others on waldorf." This website has everything one could need for Waldorf education including home-schooling Waldorf resources.

[16] The coordination of the skills classes with the main lesson classes has been missing from Waldorf educational practice. The heart-thinking aspect of Waldorf teaching is also missing from Waldorf practice. These topics were covered lightly in An Outline for a Renewal of Waldorf Education.

After reviewing Waldorf publications over the past ten years it would be fair for me to predict that the current Waldorf movement will remain a *fixed form of Waldorf education*. It will probably not strive to enhance itself. To the best of

American Waldorf and Steiner's Ideal: Waldorf education was born in post-World War I Germany. Money and food were scarce; and Steiner, nevertheless, was able to found a semi-independent private school at a time when independent schools were overseen by the German State. In founding the school, Steiner had to make compromises with the state and with his colleagues involved the project. To date, American Waldorf education means following the 1919 compromised German curriculum as closely as possible. The schools struggle not only with internal compromises that existed from Steiner's day, but also with pressure and goals from parents and society which often run contrary to the "best" interests of the students. Joseph Chilton Pearce, who normally speaks about Waldorf in glowing terms, has recently spoken about some American Waldorf schools deviating substantially from their own child-friendly goals and methods!

Self-development and spiritual hygiene in the form of exercises and meditations have all but disappeared from Waldorf teacher training, and now various Waldorf associations teach the Waldorf *pedagogical basics* in order to get teachers ready for the classroom. The compromises and questions remain the same in all countries and cultures: do our educational methods meet the demands of the child's developmental stages and tasks of our times, or are we adapting ourselves to the external demands of the state and society and pragmatic necessity? I have spoken to Waldorf teacher trainers and administrators that maintain that the inner aspects of Waldorf training have been totally neglected.

The American Waldorf Movement struggles in its identity. A school that claims that it educates children to have a *strong will*, by its own account, teaches in a very effete manner. It is not unusual for Waldorf schools to be short on boys. Another issue is that the middle school often is identical to the elementary school in method. I experienced this as a Waldorf student. As a faculty member I noticed that the high school teaching methods often did not reflect the pedagogical and social needs of high school students (the students were either spoon fed or lectured at relentlessly). Gisela O'Neil once remarked that the future of Waldorf middle and high school education could be found in aspects of the Mortimer Adler's *Paideia Program*, especially the teaching of 'great books' through the Socratic method! The Waldorf high school reps have not yet figured out the balance between an age-appropriate education, the modern consciousness of the children (vs. those children of 1920), and a curriculum which is challenging without busywork.

Steiner expected that the high school students would have real experience working in various industries. Young people always enjoy taking part in the adult world and learning about how things work. In this aspect Waldorf high schools have adjusted themselves to parental wishes, and instead of having serious non-academic working experiences, the learners simply prepare to go to competitive colleges. Waldorf schools are seeking outside recognition for their work and often publish their students' college acceptances in their brochures. Rarely do they mention the benefits of their character building education, an attribute that cannot be accessed by college acceptances and SATs (one study done suggested that Waldorf students have 37% higher moral intelligence rate than other private school students).

Are there famous Waldorf grads? According to the various Waldorf websites there are in fact *very few* famous or ingenious Waldorf graduates. Some graduates became famous actors in America and Europe, and others become significant members of the Red Army Faction in Germany, which the website does not mention (Joseph Beuys and Saul Bellow did not go to Waldorf schools). The website names a few people who did not go to Waldorf, but who sent their children there! Can the movement honestly say that their teaching unfolds the latent capacities of their students with an education towards freedom? Could you imagine Jennifer Aniston speaking her lines in that monotone way that Waldorf teachers have their kids do in their school plays?

This age calls for a radical move away from standards that are based on ideologies and pedagogies which don't arise out of useful child psychology. A reexamination of the <u>Primer</u> might help this process. It would take a lot of strength and commitment for educators to follow an educational strategy which leaves behind old school sequences and modern educational trends. The idea of a spiritually oriented education has it roots in Steiner's world view and methods, but its radical fulfillment must be found in a new organic form. Authors such as John Gatto, Joseph Chilton Pearce, Mortimer Adler, and Paul Goodman have given many concrete suggestions about freedom and education. The time has come for the new model.

---

my knowledge American Waldorf education, except for acquiring some multicultural add-ons, still has as its goal the realization of the 1919 plan set by Dr. Steiner. Its representatives and journals (*Renewal* and *Waldorf Research bulletin*) are self-congratulatory and avoid real self-analysis (Rueckschau) which Steiner said is essential to living in spirit. I expect that the future of Steiner's impulse will be found in completely new educational ideas and *practices*, and that any serious self-renewal on the part of Waldorf organization may have passed.

The Heart-Logik Teachers College: I am currently writing a proposal for a new teachers college. I would like to show what is essential in forming a school and community that is organic-living in every aspect. A new education should start with teachers who think in an integrated manner, who have developed their ability to be loving beings, and can *work together* in pursuing a general vision of a conscious community. The goal is the realization of an off-the-grid, self-sustaining community which supports technological, social, and ethical-moral innovation. An effective community gives back to the earth and society, rather than depleting and polluting it. The college faculty would model this new living, so that when the students graduate they will have mastered the skills necessary to create other organic communities.

Every new form of education starts with a renewed person. In a stressful and hectic world it is hard to find the time and patience to unfold one's higher frequency self. Thus the new teacher might need several years to unfold in a quiet atmosphere and to release all energetic and psychological 'stuck-ness.' One way to facilitate this process is to use various self-clearing methods such as the "empathic healing path" developed by Noa Batlin. This path is safe and excellent for moving on energetic and psychological 'stuck-ness.' Once completed others notice the changes. For example, young children would feel and say that "Ms. Jones has very nice energy." And because Ms. Jones has worked on herself and prepared herself for a new way of living, her work with others could be done with new clarity. The new school does not teach, but models what it means to live on a higher frequency of love and life.

The new teacher training will arise naturally out of organic thinking. Steiner mastered interdisciplinary thought and unified the competing academic disciplines through his organic method. The organic method of thinking Steiner practiced in his writings heals the current divide between the various disciplines. Through intense study teachers will learn how to organize their thoughts in tableau form, ("tableau" meaning, they see all their ideas in one great picture), and how to apply this tableau thinking to everything they do. From the work in organic thinking the fragmentation of the Western mind and its academic disciplines will be healed as well as the social difficulties which prevent individuals from working together. The mission of the college is to present a unified and organic curriculum, that is in and of itself, a healing experience. Steiner's main book is The Philosophy of Freehood and its study is the basis of this new organic thinking. It provides a healthy world view about the power of the human mind and freedom; and provides an organic form of thinking that aids greatly in the practice of intuition. The idea behind the school must be an organic-living idea before the school can be in praxis a living whole.

The college courses will be coordinated so that their *actual* purpose is fulfilled. Poetry needs to be recited, practiced, and related to music and other disciplines, not simply criticized/analyzed as is the case now in our learning institutions. Science courses should be applicable to the real world, for example biology will aid us in understanding plant energies, in renewing our environment, medicine, and food quality. What is the use of political philosophy if it does not allow us to understand the form, strengths, and shortcomings of our system; if it doesn't teach us how to be just and to be active in political renewal? Every discipline has its own particular magic. The true role of academic study is for us to find joy in ideas; and for us to know that ideas have the ability to explain and reconnect us to the essence of things around us and even to ourselves. A modified list of great books is only one aspect of study which is uplifting; the other aspect is the implementation of those ideas in the real world. A true college education gives students skills which helps them orient them through life. The great books help us decipher the world, the sciences, and personal relationships; the artistic classes pave the way for a true aesthetic and moral sense; the life skill classes give the students opportunities and preparation for the economy in that they know how things function in practical life.

To balance the academics, life skill classes such as house building, cooking healthily, growing food, and learning to produce energy will be a part of the curriculum. Corporate colleges make us into consumers, but a new spirit in our institutions can lead us to a new organic way of living. Other practical subjects are meditation, spiritual movement, and healing arts. These things will be part of the future college experience.

There must be some form of healing/recovery place where teachers have time to enter into a new way of living and thinking. For those individuals who are not already teachers, they could attend the college and learn an organic way of living from the beginning. Once there are enough individuals who have committed themselves to living in a loving way, then a high school and elementary school could be formed. The proposal will also cover a general outline of teaching strategies for a new high school and elementary school.

Bibliography

Mortimer Alder, How to Read a Book is an important contribution to working with organic thinking.

Florin Lowndes, The Enlivening of the Chakra of the Heart and Das Erwecken Des Herzdenkens. These texts are continuations and elaborations of O'Neil's original work. Lowndes also has in his possession the O'Neil legacy. Lowndes has reworked a handful of heart-thinking German edition on his website: www.heartthink.de

George O'Neil, "A Study-book to the Philosophy of Spiritual Activity" available at Rudolf Steiner Library (mimeograph) or at www.organicthinking.org. This is the first available manuscript (1961) on the heart-thinking in Rudolf Steiner's work. O'Neil sent it out to many Anthroposophists who were mystified by its contents. Photocopies of the original are very popular according to the librarians at Steiner Library. O'Neil also wrote a series of articles in the Anthroposophical Newsletter on *How to Read Steiner's* Knowledge of Higher Worlds and its Attainment.

O'Neil worked out the archetype of the human biography in his The Human Life. The book is available but the *indifferent* publisher, Mercury Press, does not promote the book, and it often appears on Amazon.com as "out of print."

Mark Riccio, An Outline for a Renewal of Waldorf Education (self-published), available at Steiner College Bookstore, www.waldorfbooks.com, and the Goetheanum Bookstore. This booklet expanded Florin Lowndes' original article submitted to the Pedagogical Section leader Heinz Zimmermann at the Goetheanum. The Pedagogical Section rejected Lowndes' work and stated that they were not interested, as Waldorf researchers, in "a systematic approach" to Steiner's work. The booklet attempts to show that the Waldorf curriculum and teaching methods in theory are based on heart-thinking and that the future of Waldorf depends on the re-enlivening of the training of future Waldorf teachers.

Made in the USA
Monee, IL
01 August 2021